NEW FOREST COOKERY

Traditional Recipes from a Forest Cabin

New Forest Cookery

TRADITIONAL RECIPES FROM A FOREST CABIN

IRENE SOPER

ARCADY BOOKS
Ashurst, Southampton

First Edition 1983

ARCADY BOOKS LTD
2 Woodlands Road,
Ashurst,
Southampton,
Hampshire, SO4 2AD

ISBN 0 907753 06 X

Illustrations by Arthur Soper

Designed and produced by
Brian Masterton and Associates Limited,
Whittington House,
64 High Street,
Fareham,
Hampshire, PO16 7BG

Printed in England by
Alresford Printing Works,
The Dean,
Alresford,
Hampshire, SO24 9BD

ACKNOWLEDGEMENTS

I WOULD like to thank my kind New Forest neighbours for their help in giving me traditional recipes which had been passed on in their families, and the many Forest folk who not only entertained me with stories from yesterday but also gave me material for my book.

My thanks also to Juliette de Baïracli Levy, whose book *'Wanderers in the New Forest'* published by Faber and Faber, was written in the Cabin, for allowing me to reproduce some of the unusual dishes she made during her stay there.

Finally, I thank my husband who illustrated my book and acted as my not unwilling guinea-pig while I tried out these recipes.

Irene Soper

PREFACE

THIS collection of traditional recipes from the New Forest naturally includes many ingredients once available from the Forest itself. Nowadays the Forest byelaws prohibit the removal of plants and animals from the area but most of the ingredients can be easily purchased especially from local shops. Some of the very old recipes which included contents now difficult to obtain have been adapted to make them suitable for the modern cook. Take care when cooking wild berries and fruits and be sure to distinguish between edible and poisonous fungi. If in any doubt, I would recommend reading *Mushrooms and Fungi* by Moira Savonius, published by Octopus Books, London, and Bounty Books, New York.

CONTENTS

A NOTE ON OVEN TEMPERATURES

The majority of these recipes were originally intended for an open fire. They have been adapted for modern use. Consult the table below as a guide to correct oven temperatures.

	Electric	Gas
Very Cool	250 - 275	¼ - ¾
Cool	290 - 325	1 - 2
Moderate	350 - 400	3, 4, 5
Mod. Hot	425	6
Hot	450 - 475	7, 8
Very Hot	500 - 550	9 - 12

INTRODUCTION

IT was after we moved to our cottage in the New Forest that we discovered the old cabin tucked away in a corner of the wild garden, half hidden by overgrown laurels and a spreading yew tree, to be an original Forest dwelling. Built of clay and cob with a roof of thatch it is said to be over three hundred years old. It is one of the few remaining in the Forest now, as most have fallen into disrepair. The outside walls then were pale pink, and the thatch that was badly in need of restoring was of heather and reeds from the water-meadow beyond the garden. Inside the cabin is one large downstairs room with an open fireplace on one side of which the bricks are smooth and rounded, possibly made so by the resting backs of generations of foresters as they sat beside the glowing embers. In the opposite wall is the remains of an old baking oven. Suspended from a beam halfway up the chimney hangs a chain with a hook on the end, on which many pots of stew have cooked over the open fire, or sides of bacon hung to cure in the smoke of burning gorse faggots.

In the past the cabin has been lived in and visited by foresters, artists, and gypsies; the last person to live there was herbalist Juliette de Baïracli Levy. It is surrounded on three sides by forest with magnificent views across the wide expanses of heather and gorse and gentle sloping peat bogs. The tiny rear window looks out upon a water-meadow where wild iris and kingcups grow. Outside in the lane the ponies come and go stopping briefly to drink at the well. All day long in springtime the cuckoos fly and call around the cabin, and at dusk from its heathy cover the purring trill of the nightjar can be heard as it vibrates on the evening breeze. As darkness envelops the garden around the cabin the nocturnal creatures venture abroad, an owl hoots from its hollow tree, and the sharp scream of a fox pierces the night air.

Looking at the primitive surroundings inside the cabin with its small alcove kitchen, I wondered how the Forest folk managed in the days before modern transport, freezers, and cookers. For here in the Forest, often in remote places, are farmhouses and cottages unaltered for hundreds of years. They stand exposed to all weathers, the summer winds heavy with the scent of heather and honey from the hives, the lashing rains of autumn, and the snow storms of winter when they were often cut off for days. I decided to discover more about this aspect of Forest life and also present day happenings by talking to, and questioning as many people as I could who live around us. I soon found that in these old farmsteads and cottages there were many Forest recipes which had been handed down from one generation to another. Some are still used whilst others, written down on scraps of paper, the handwriting sometimes faded and difficult to read, lay forgotten in drawers and cupboards. Recipes that were not recorded only passed by word of mouth were the most difficult ones to set down, but I have made every effort to be as accurate as possible. The others I have copied in their original wording. Some are very old. The rest are everyday Forest recipes. recipes. Notes in brackets make the recipes clear for a modern cook to follow.

Many pleasant hours I have spent in search of these treasures which brought me in contact with many interesting characters, particularly the foresters who recall so well stories of olden days. Gypsies too have been my visitors also remembering their days camping 'on the Forest' and cooking around a campfire.

Our own cottage and cabin nestle on the side of a hill. Outside the gate we have the wells* of Abbots Well with their cool clear water which I often use for cooking. We make our own wine and bake our own bread. Despite a modern cooker some of the following recipes I cook in their original way on the open fire of the old cabin burning sweet smelling gorse wood instead of logs. But the mouth-watering flavours of the past can be captured in a modern kitchen as I am sure you will discover if you enter the world of New Forest cookery.

Irene Soper
Abbots Well

---

* We refer to 'the wells' at Abbots Well as there are two separate drinking places fed by one spring. One well, protected by a cover in recent years, is used for human consumption. The other in the form of a sunken barrel provides the Forest animals with refreshment along the way. The Well is reputed to have Roman origins but is certainly mentioned in New Forest chronicles as early as 1217.

ON THE FOREST

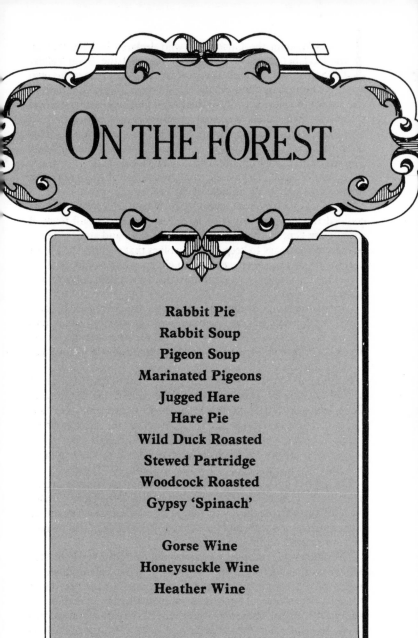

Rabbit Pie
Rabbit Soup
Pigeon Soup
Marinated Pigeons
Jugged Hare
Hare Pie
Wild Duck Roasted
Stewed Partridge
Woodcock Roasted
Gypsy 'Spinach'

Gorse Wine
Honeysuckle Wine
Heather Wine

IT was William the Conqueror who declared in 1079 that all the land between Southampton Water and the Avon Valley, the Solent and the Wiltshire Downs, was in future to be his own exclusive hunting ground. So the 'New Forest' was established. In the days of the Normans life in the Forest for the peasant, or churl as he was then called, was very primitive. His hut was built of wattle and daub on a wood frame, and the floors were of mud. This dwelling consisted of only one room and possessed no windows. The only light came from the open door and a hole in the roof where the smoke escaped. The smoke came from a fire of sticks burnt on the hearth-stone in the middle of the room.

The churl usually kept a few swine which at certain times he could drive into the woods to feed. Sometimes a small flock of sheep were kept in rough pens built of hurdles and stones. These pens were necessary to keep out the wolves that roamed the Forest in those days. The sheep were fed on chopped leaves and meal. At the end of the year most of them were killed and salted down for the winter.

Around the hut protected by thick hedges the churl grew his own rye. From this he made rye bread and rye-cake which he sometimes toasted in the embers. With the rye bread the churl and his family drank hot milk from earthen bowls. With his meat he drank mead or a rather flat ale.

In subsequent years the peasant and forester had an abundance of food on their doorstep, and could live entirely 'on the Forest'. They had game, wild herbs, fungi, berries and nuts at their disposal. Some possessed the common right of turbary which enabled them to collect fuel for their fires. Although most of the older Forest recipes were cooked over an open fire, some cottages had peat ovens, which burnt the turf cut from the Forest.

The gypsies until modern times were allowed to camp and roam freely in the Forest. Their colourful vans used to be parked under the holly trees across the heath, not far from our house. They filled their cooking pots with rabbits, squirrels, hedgehogs, wild onions, wild watercress, and other herbs.

The rabbit was perhaps the most popular food from the Forest for both peasant and gypsy alike. The gypsies used to catch rabbits by means of a net after dark; the nets were placed near the rabbit burrows, dogs were sent out and the rabbits, cut off from their holes, were easily caught. These nets were made by the gypsy women with string, some were several yards long. The Romany just cooked his rabbit together with wild onions in his stew pot. The peasant preferred his made into a pie.

14

RABBIT PIE

One rabbit, half a pound of bacon, two hard boiled eggs, one small onion, half a teaspoonful of mixed herbs, seasoning, one tablespoonful of flour, half a pint of stock, and pastry crust.

Cut the rabbit into joints, dip in seasoned flour, and fry until golden brown in a little hot fat. Place in a pie-dish with slices of eggs and strips of bacon. Sprinkle in more seasoning and herbs. Pour in stock. Cover with pastry and bake for about two hours in a moderate oven. Do not forget to leave a hole in the pastry to allow the steam to escape.

RABBIT SOUP

Joint *one rabbit,* put into a pan with *two quarts of cold water,* bring to the boil and skim well, add *one carrot and one onion* (sliced), *two stalks of celery, a bunch of sweet herbs,** and *half a teaspoonful of peppercorns, a little ham, and two or three cloves;* simmer gently for one and a half hours, lift out the back of the rabbit, remove flesh from bones and put bones back into pan; let the simmering continue for one hour longer, pour stock through fine sieve. Melt *two ounces of butter* in a pan, stir into it *two ounces of flour* till smooth, add the stock and stir until it boils. Add now *a little salt, one glass of port wine, a tablespoonful of mushroom ketchup**; also the flesh from the back of the rabbit cut into small pieces. Serve with toast or fried sippets of bread.

*SWEET HERBS

Two or three sprigs of parsley, mint, marjoram, sage, and thyme. Tie these together for easy removal during or after cooking.

*MUSHROOM KETCHUP

Four pounds of large fresh mushrooms, three ounces of salt, half an ounce of whole ginger, small piece of mace, four cloves, quarter of an ounce of pepper.

Make sure the mushrooms are quite free from insects. Wash them in cold water in a colander under a gently running tap. Drain well. Break them into small pieces, and put them in a large casserole with the salt sprinkled among them. Cover with a lid or plate and stand in a warm spot or at the side of a stove. They must be warm, but must not cook at all. Leave for twenty-four hours. Then strain off the liquor, pressing the mushrooms to obtain as much as possible. Put liquor into a pan and boil gently for thirty minutes. Add the spices tied in muslin. Boil again for thirty minutes. Take out the spices and when the ketchup is cold, strain, bottle, and seal.

Large flocks of wood pigeons flap from one wood to another in the Forest, often descending on vegetable patches in the cottage gardens and devouring everything. So it seems only right that they also provided food for the pot! Today pigeons can be obtained from local shops.

PIGEON SOUP
This is a very old recipe dated 1895

Cut up *one pound of lean beef* into small pieces, put these into a pan, with *five pints of cold water,* also *four pigeons* cut in halves lengthwise, bring to the boil and skim thoroughly; slice *one large onion, two good size carrots, one turnip* and *a stick of celery* and add together with *one teaspoon of peppercorns,* and *a bunch of sweet herbs.* Boil gently for half an hour, remove the pigeons and continue the boiling for one and a half hours more. Remove the breasts from the pigeons, cut up into small cubes and set aside; take the meat from the legs, pound into a mortar until smooth, rub through a wire sieve. Put into a pan *one ounce of butter,* melt, and add *one ounce of flour,* also pulp of pigeon legs, then stock which should be strained, breasts of pigeons, and *one tablespoonful of lemon juice* and *salt* to taste. Re-heat and serve.

MARINATED PIGEONS

Before cooking, older birds were marinated for at least two days. Bay leaves were used in this dish as they are in so many Forest recipes. Most New Forest cottagers grew bay trees by their front doors as they believed the bay kept bad luck away!
Slice *a large onion* and put it into a shallow dish with *two bay leaves, half a teaspoonful of peppercorns,* and *a wineglassful of*

malt vinegar. Lay *two pigeons* in this marinade and turn and baste them twice a day for two days. If the birds are old you should leave them in the marinade for a day longer. Take them up, wipe them dry, and lard the breasts evenly, then put them in a saucepan with *an ounce of butter,* and turn them over a moderate fire (burner) until they are equally browned — about five minutes. Lift them out, stir *a dessertspoonful of flour* in with the butter, and mix it briskly with a wooden spoon until it begins to colour, then add *four ounces of fat bacon* cut into small pieces, the *chopped liver of the birds, a medium cupful of stock or water,* the strained *juice of half a lemon with an inch or so of the rind,* and *a little pepper, salt, and grated nutmeg.*

Let this sauce boil, then put in the pigeons, cover them closely, and let them stew for half an hour. Serve the birds on a hot dish with the sauce poured round them.

At one time hares were more in evidence in the Forest than they are now. Although still hunted by beagles I doubt very much if they are often lucky enough to find any. Dating back to the days when hares were more prolific comes this recipe.

JUGGED HARE

This recipe was dated 1884 and I give it in full. Of course today we can buy our hare ready dressed.

A hare, some good stock, about two or three pints of water in proportion to the size of the hare; *a small onion stuck with cloves; some lemon peel; pepper and salt; some forcemeat balls; a glass of port wine; some butter, lard, or dripping.*

The entrails, liver etc of a hare should be removed as soon as it is received; after doing this, wipe the inside, pepper it well, and hang up the hare. When wanted for dressing, skin it and truss as if for roasting, then half roast it before a clear fire (in a moderate oven) from half an hour to an hour being enough, according to the size of the hare. Baste constantly while the hare is roasting. Then cut it up into small pieces, and put these into an earthen jar with a cover (casserole dish) pouring sufficient stock over them to nearly cover them, and adding the onion, lemon peel, salt etc. Put the jar into a very cool oven, and allow the contents to simmer for two and a half or three hours, according to the size of the hare. When sufficiently done, take out the pieces of hare and pour the gravy into a clean saucepan, adding a little more stock, if necessary, and the port wine. If not sufficiently seasoned, put a little more pepper and salt. When the gravy is just about to boil pour it over the pieces of hare, which should have been placed in a very hot dish, and send to the table as quickly as possible accompanied by forcemeat balls.

HARE PIE

Skin *the hare,* cut it into convenient size joints, season these with *pepper and two pounded cloves,* and fry them in *hot butter* for ten or fifteen minutes, then put them aside to cool.

Pound *the liver* in a mortar with *four ounces of bacon, a shallot finely minced, a teaspoon of parsley, a teaspoonful of thyme and half a teaspoon of pepper.* Whilst pounding, add *a glass of port* till the forcemeat is of the proper consistency. The head, trimmings, and inferior parts may be stewed for gravy with the same seasoning which would be used for jugged hare. Line the edge of a pie-dish with good crust, arrange the hare and forcemeat inside it in alternate layers, cover the whole with *thin slices of bacon,* and pour over it *half a pint of gravy,* to which has been added *a teaspoonful of redcurrant jelly, and if liked a glass of port.* Bake in a moderate oven for 1½ hours and serve hot.

THE open expanses of heathland in the Forest consist of acres of heather and gorse clumps; sometimes with a stream meandering through that opens out here and there into a series of small ponds where it meets the boggy areas. These are the wild places of the Forest, impossible to walk through. They abound with wild life. Bog myrtle scents the air with its pungent fragrance, the curlews and redshank call. Even a snipe may rise from the marshes and go worrying into the air. It is in these secret places that the wild duck still live as they did in olden times. Wild duck love the bogs and small rushy pools to be found on the heath and moorlands of the Forest. Their favourite nesting place is often away from the water amongst the heather and gorse. I once disturbed a pair in the thick bracken of a woodland glade.

A story was told to me by an old forester neighbour of how two gypsy girls he knew were walking in the Forest when they came upon a wild duck on a pond. One girl jumped fully clothed into the water and caught the astonished duck before it realised what was happening. That night it was much enjoyed in the cooking pot back at the gypsy camp. He goes on to tell of how the gypsy boys often caught wild duck for the cooking pot. Only they used slings and stones and sometimes bows and arrows.

The peasant also enjoyed an occasional wild duck from a Forest pool, but his would probably have been roasted in an oven or before the open fire.

WILD DUCK ROASTED

Wild duck can be obtained from shops when in season from 1 September to 28 February. This is an old recipe given in full. Pluck, draw, and truss the bird. Roast it before a fierce fire (in a very hot oven) for about fifteen minutes. Send *cut lemon* to the table with it, and *cayenne pepper*. Wild duck requires no gravy. It should be red inside when cut. The breast is the best part. In carving a wild duck it is customary for the carver to score the breast into slices down the bone, and squeeze lemon and cayenne pepper into the gashes.

Another bird almost sure to be found running close to the ground between the heather was the partridge. It was so well camouflaged by its plumage of colours blending with the wild surroundings that it did not often fall prey to the hunter. So on such times as it did it was considered a delicacy.

STEWED PARTRIDGE

These may be obtained from shops between the 1 September and 1 February. *A brace of partridge, two ounces of butter, half a pint of water, wineglass of white wine, one small onion sliced, chopped sweet herbs, salt and pepper.*

Drawn and clean the birds, divide into pieces and fry to a light brown in the butter, sprinkle with a *teaspoonful of flour,* add the onions, herbs, water, and pepper, simmer half an hour or until tender; lift out the pieces of partridge, skim off the fat from gravy, boil until reduced to half the quantity, add the wine and salt, strain over the bird and serve. Garnish the dish with *pieces of lemon.*

The woodcock was an occasional dish for the forester with a gun. Being an elusive bird that circled around the tree tops at dusk croaking as it went it was considered a prize if the forester managed to shoot one. Having done so it was so small it was eaten on a piece of toast.

WOODCOCK ROASTED
(available in season)

Truss the bird, roast it before a fierce fire, or in a hot oven for fifteen to twenty minutes. Place a piece of toast underneath the bird after it has been roasted for a few minutes to catch the trail; baste frequently. Let the butter with which the bird is basted soak into the toast. The bird should be served on toast immediately it is roasted, with a good unflavoured gravy, and some bread sauce. The woodcock should be red inside when it is cut, and bright brown outside, the fire or oven must be very hot.

The number of nettles growing in the Forest every spring probably accounted for the gypsies using them for making their spinach. This recipe originated from the cabin in my garden where gypsies once were frequent visitors.

GYPSY SPINACH
(Boiled nettles)

Wearing stout gloves, gather some *young nettles* (you need a large bunch to feed two people) and cook for several minutes in *boiling salty water,* until soft. Sprinkle with any *flaked cereals* you wish — oats or wheat germ are very good — *a little butter* or *some grated white cheese.* To enhance the taste add a few wild onions. (Substitute *chopped chives* or *spring onions).* This is a springtime dish when the nettles are young and tender.

Another springtime dish of the gypsies in the days when they camped on the Forest was young bracken fronds. These were tied in little bundles, cooked until tender in boiling salty water and eaten dipped in melted butter.

The Forest provided a wealth of ingredients for making wine. Amongst them was the wild mint which the peasant used to make a cordial which he called 'hum water'. Here are some recipes for delightful wines made from the most prolific of our wild plants.

GORSE WINE

In springtime the gorse spreads its yellow mantle over the wild heathland of the Forest and fills the air with its heady coconut scent. The bees can only reach the pollen of this beautiful golden flower, the nectar being secured inside their cups. By gathering these flowers complete with nectar a wine as sweet as honey mead can be brewed.

Gather *five pounds of gorse flowers,* and put them into a pan. Boil a *gallon of water* together with *three pounds of sugar* and *the rinds and juice of two lemons and two oranges,* skim and pour over the flowers, add *half an ounce of dry yeast.* Cover and allow to work for three days skimming each day, strain carefully and pour liquid into a cask, and fit airlock, when working has stopped top up with water to which *a little sugar* has been added, cork down, and bottle the following year when the gorse is once again in flower.

HONEYSUCKLE WINE

In summer honeysuckle can be found everywhere in the Forest, climbing over the tops of bushes to bathe in the sunshine, delicately hanging over a Forest pool trailing its blossoms in the cool water, or in the deep Forest falling in drifts from the trunks of larger trees having given up the upward climb to try and reach the sunlight. As evening approaches the fragrance of the honeysuckle grows stronger attracting the long tongued moths, and the White Admiral butterfly for which it provides its favourite food.

Two pints of honeysuckle blossom, three pounds of sugar, four ounces of raisins, one lemon, one orange, one campden tablet, one tablespoon grape tannin, one gallon of water, ½ ounce of dry yeast.

The flowers must be fully open and dry, wash them, pour the water over them and stir in two pounds of sugar, the minced raisins and lemon and orange juice, crush the campden tablet and stir in, leave to stand overnight, then add the tannin and yeast.

Put in a warm place and leave to ferment for a week stirring each day, then add the remaining sugar and stir well. Strain into a jar with airlock, and leave until it has ceased to bubble, then strain into bottles and cork down.

HEATHER WINE

As summer deepens the open Forest is covered by a purple carpet of intricate and subtle shades on a green ground. By picking the heather flowers to capture their fragrance the forester was able to produce a wine as fresh and sweet as the air that blows over the Forest.

Fill a saucepan with *heather flowers* in full bloom, cover with water and boil for an hour, strain, and leave to cool, measure the liquid, and add the *juice of two oranges and one lemon.* To each gallon of liquid add *three pounds of sugar.* Stir well, add *three quarters of an ounce of dry yeast* mixed with a little of the liquid. Put into a fermenting jar, insert airlock. When fermenting has finished, bottle, and keep for several months to mature.

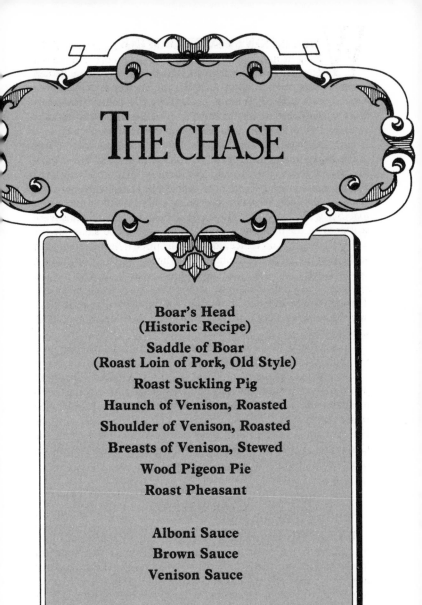

THE CHASE

Boar's Head
(Historic Recipe)

Saddle of Boar
(Roast Loin of Pork, Old Style)

Roast Suckling Pig

Haunch of Venison, Roasted

Shoulder of Venison, Roasted

Breasts of Venison, Stewed

Wood Pigeon Pie

Roast Pheasant

Alboni Sauce

Brown Sauce

Venison Sauce

23

WHEN the New Forest became the hunting ground of the King he and his nobles hunted the wild boar and the red deer. It must have been a colourful sight as the huntsmen on horseback came crashing through the bracken in full cry, the vivid colours of their tunics and cloaks, purple, gold, crimson and blue, splashed against the dense green of the undergrowth, with the sudden glint of sunlight on a spear-point or buckle.

After the chase, the hunting party would return to a lodge or one of the Forest manor houses for refreshment. The hall of a typical manor house was solidly built of stone with narrow unglazed windows and overhead rafters of timber blackened with soot from the fire below. On the walls were hung a few brightly woven rugs, together with weapons of the chase and of war. Some skins were scattered on the floor and a heavy trestle table stood alongside the wall with benches on either side. Two or three tallow dips stood in sockets on the middle of the table. Overhead a lantern hung from a beam, caught by every draught which spun it around casting alternate light and darkness across the noisy revellers below. Through a haze of smoke would come the rich scent of roasting flesh and the sweet smell of cider brimming over the horn-shaped silver mugs.

During the reign of King Charles the hunting feast had become a more pompous occasion.

The highlight of the evening was the entrance of the boar's head upon a silver platter, looking both ferocious and frivolous with menacing tusks and a flower tucked behind one ear. The following recipe was found in a farmhouse on the estate of one of the last of the Forest manors to the north west that was held by William the Conqueror. I include it here mainly for its historic value but you could, of course, try it with a pig's head.

BOAR'S HEAD

Take a good *boar's head* and wash it thoroughly before splitting it in half from the back forwards; do not damage the snout or forehead. Cut out the brains, the tongue and the bone. Soak the head in a brine bath made from a *quarter of a pound of rock salt to one gallon of water,* and leave for two days. Boil the *tongue* slowly for one hour or until tender, skin and leave aside. Take the head out of the brine rinse and dry thoroughly, put to one side. With a sharp knife lift off the *fillets from the backs of four young rabbits,* and strip the rest of the meat from the bones. Put the fillets in a dish with a *gill of sherry, three shallots finely chopped, three bay leaves, quarter of a teaspoonful of alspice, salt and black pepper,* leave for four hours. *Mince the remainder of the rabbit meat* and mix with a *pound of lean minced veal, and a pound of minced liver.* Add the *sherry marinade* after removing the bay leaves, and add more seasoning to taste. Cut the tongue into strips the same size as the rabbit fillets.

Spread the forcemeat over the boar's head and on top place the rabbit and tongue strips. Scatter *half an ounce of blanched and crushed pistachio nuts, and one small shredded truffle* (if available) over this and shape up the forcemeat and head. Sew up completely, wrap in muslin, or cotton, and bind the snout, leaving the whole head in its original shape. Put into a large saucepan with the bones, cover with water, add vegetables and *bouquet garni.* Bring slowly to the boil and simmer gently for four hours. Remove from the saucepan, tighten the cloth, press and hold securely with weights and boards to preserve the shape. Leave in a cool place overnight. Remove the cloth, glaze, and decorate.

To Glaze the Boar's Head

Brush over the whole head with a *savoury jelly**, allow to dry and repeat the process until the required thickness is obtained.

*Boil some bone stock until it is syrupy in texture and add gelatine to make it set.

The decoration of the head is traditional in England. Hard boiled white of egg and truffle (or mushrooms) are used for the eyes. Tusks are represented by celery and a bright flower should be tucked behind the ear. The head rests on a mound of rice and is ringed around with bay or rosemary.

The flesh of the young boar was considered a delicacy. This is an old recipe for saddle of boar which can easily be adapted for modern use. Try it using loin of pork.

SADDLE OF BOAR
(Roast Loin of Pork, old style)

Take one pint of cider, one small onion peeled and chopped, three bay leaves, three cloves, half a teaspoonful of salt, black pepper, two ounces of butter and a few peppercorns.

Put the ingredients together in a saucepan and bring to the boil. Leave to cool, then strain and pour over the joint. Leave for twenty four hours. Turn the joint occasionally and baste thoroughly. Cook the joint in *butter* over a gentle fire (burner) until browned, using some of the marinade to keep it basted. Cover and simmer slowly for two hours.

Prepare a sauce by cutting the *rind from two oranges.* Slice the rind. Rub *three lumps of sugar* on the oranges. Put the sugar into a basin with *six tablespoons of red currant jelly, a little white pepper, one chopped shallot, one spoonful of mixed mustard* and enough *port wine* to make the sauce as thick as a good cream; add the orange rind which should be cut very thin, heat gently in a saucepan, then pour over the carved slices of the joint. Serve with *wild apple jelly*.*

SUCKLING PIG

Roast suckling pig was served on special occasions accompanied by the wild boar and a wood pigeon pie. Today, if you give your butcher some warning, he will probably be able to get you a suckling pig which you can roast for a celebration dinner or barbecue.

Thoroughly *clean the pig* (which should not be more than six weeks old) and scrape the whole surface, stuff it with a *sage and onion stuffing;* truss and skewer. Put the pig in a large baking tin, rub it over with *clarified butter or olive oil, sprinkle with pepper and salt.* Pour *a pint of hot water* into the pan with the pig, cover the pig with *buttered paper* or aluminium foil. Bake in a hot oven (about 400) allowing 25 to 30 minutes per pound. Remove paper or foil 15 minutes before end of cooking time, dish up whole and serve with *wild apple jelly.**

*See Recipe page 71

I have a very old recipe for cooking a larger suckling pig on a spit. The pig was prepared in the same way, then, the recipe reads: 'put it before a clear brisk fire. Baste constantly, or the crackling will be blistered and burnt, instead of crisp and brown. As the middle part requires less roasting than the ends, it is usual when the pig is half done, to hang a flat iron from the spit in such a position that it will shade the heat of the fire from the middle. Cut the head off before removing from the fire. To dish it cut the pig open, and lay the sides back to back, lengthwise, upon the dish, with one half of the head at each end and the ears at the sides. Serve with a rich brown gravy, a sharp apple sauce or currant sauce. Time to roast according to size; a three week old pig, two hours.'

THE New Forest is famed for its venison. Hunting the red deer in the Forest first began in the reign of William the Conqueror and continued till the Deer Removal Act in 1851. During this period a lot of poaching was also carried out, often by cruel means, such as an apple on a hook hanging from a tree. A story told by an old forester neighbour of ours was that he could remember a man once living in Abbots Well Cottage who having shot a deer dragged it indoors and hid it in bed with his wife. When the police arrived they were unable to find anything as they did not think of searching the bed. He went on to tell of another man who killed a deer and brought it indoors and put it in front of the fire. His wife fetched blankets and pillows covered it over and put her two small children on top and told them to 'bide quiet till the police had gone'.

The gypsies also would poach but by a different method; they would stalk the deer and hide behind trees, jumping out on the deer and killing them. An old gypsy lady told me she could remember as a child sitting around a campfire in the Forest eating deer stew; that was in the days when the gypsies roamed the Forest and were allowed to pitch camp there. Although she still lives in a caravan in the Forest it is on a permanent site. She says she still has her old bender tent, cooking pot and kettle from her earlier days.

The red deer are no longer hunted in the New Forest; there are only two small herds surviving. The fallow deer are numerous and as well as being hunted they are periodically shot to control their numbers; this is called culling. During the hard winter months potatoes are fed to the deer in certain enclosures. Unfortunately this practice although providing the much needed food encourages the deer to become tame, losing their natural fear of man, making them easy prey to the poachers; as poaching alas is still carried out in the Forest. Perhaps the method used by the keepers of cutting holly branches down to the ground for the deer to browse is the best way of providing the food.

There is no excuse for poaching these days as quite a number of New Forest butchers sell venison at very reasonable prices. Although the red deer venison is no longer obtainable the venison of the fallow deer is considered almost as good. The butcher selling the widest range of venison is at Lyndhurst, here you can buy anything from a haunch, to venison pate, faggots, and even sausages.

Venison was always allowed to hang for a week before cooking, sometimes it was left for two or three weeks. To prevent it becoming flyblown, it was rubbed immediately after skinning with flour, mixed with powdered ginger and pepper. The furrow of the backbone was dressed well with pepper. It was then wrapped in butter muslin before hanging in the larder, but every day it was inspected and given a fresh coat of flour and ginger when necessary.

HAUNCH OF ROAST VENISON
Before cooking it is wise to marinade the joint

Soak the venison for three days in the following marinade, turning it daily. *Three pints of red wine, one pint of vinegar, half a pint of olive oil, one medium size onion sliced, a clove of garlic, one sprig of rosemary, one bayleaf, peppercorns and a few cloves.*

Brush the prepared haunch with *melted butter,* and *sprinkle with pepper and salt.* Make a *flour and water paste,* knead well, then roll out a piece large enough to cover the roast. Roll round and bake in a moderate oven for three or four hours according to size of joint. When cooked, chip off paste and return joint to a very hot oven to brown.

Serve with Alboni sauce.

ALBONI SAUCE

The basis of this delicious accompaniment for venison is a good Brown Sauce. Make your Brown Sauce by cooking *four ounces of butter* in a saucepan until it browns, then add *one tablespoonful chopped parsley, two tablespoonfuls vinegar, salt and pepper.* Simmer for one minute. To make Alboni Sauce add *a large tablespoonful of redcurrant jelly* and a few *roasted beech nuts.*

ROAST SHOULDER OF VENISON

Cover the venison with *buttered or oiled paper.* Place in a hot oven. When nearly cooked (about one and a half hours) remove the paper, *flour the meat,* baste it with *butter* and brown it in a very hot oven (about half an hour) making it froth. (Venison requires a quick fire or hot oven).

When there is but little fat to the venison, it should be covered with *thin slices of mutton fat,* tied on under the buttered paper.

Serve roast potatoes with it, French beans and redcurrant jelly or venison sauce.

VENISON SAUCE

Melt a large tablespoonful of redcurrant jelly in a small stewpan. *Add six cloves, a little piece of cinnamon,* and add a *tablespoonful of port wine.* Make it just warm.

STEWED BREASTS OF VENISON

Cut up the *breasts of venison* into small pieces, *flour* these, and fry them in *butter* with *three or four sliced onions* and a *small amount of bacon* cut into cubes. When the meat is lightly browned, drain off part of the fat, and pour over the meat a *cupful of stock* and a *glassful of port,* and add a *bunch of sweet herbs, half a teaspoonful of anchovy essence and a little pepper and salt.* Simmer over a gentle heat until the venison is tender (about 30 mins.). Put the meat on a dish, strain and skim the gravy, and pour it round the venison. Garnish with *chopped stewed mushrooms.*

A rather grotesque-looking pie would also be found on the banqueting table.

WOOD PIGEON PIE

Two pigeons, half a pound of stewing steak, four slices of lean bacon and one onion.

First cut the steak into small strips, slice the onion, season and put into a saucepan, cover with water and simmer for an hour, keeping the water topped up. Strain, keeping the liquid for stock. Cut the two pigeons into four pieces and place in a pie dish with steak, bacon cut into strips, in layers, season well, and pour in stock until three quarters full. Put on pastry cover, bake in a hot oven until the pastry is risen and set, then cook at a low (cool) temperature for about one hour.

Have ready two pigeon's feet, scalded and the toes cut off, also the remainder of the stock. Before serving pour in the stock through a hole in the centre of the pie, and replace the pastry, ornament with the feet, fixing them in a nearly upright position.

The pie may be served either hot or cold; if the latter the stock must be sufficiently strong to form a jelly when cold.

In medieval times pigs were used to find and dig up truffles in the New Forest. The truffles were plentiful and used quite freely in cooking. Today they are extremely expensive but sometimes other ingredients can be substituted for them. Try this recipe using mushrooms or chestnuts.

ROAST PHEASANT
STUFFED WITH TRUFFLES
(Mushrooms or Chestnuts)

One pheasant, two or three truffles (or a quarter of a pound of mushrooms or chestnuts), one teaspoon minced parsley, one tablespoonful of breadcrumbs, three shallots, bunch of sweet herbs, one egg, one and a half ounces of butter, one glass of red wine, one dessertspoonful of lemon juice, quarter of a pint of water, one teaspoonful of flour, salt and pepper.

Prepare a forcemeat of half the truffles (or substitute), one shallot, the seasoning, breadcrumbs and parsley, mince all together and mix with the egg, adding also the liver of the bird, first minced and fried. Draw and truss the pheasant, fill the breast with the forcemeat; now *lard* the breast, cover the whole with *thin slices of bacon* and roast in a moderate oven about forty-five to sixty minutes, according to size. About five minutes before it is ready, remove the bacon to allow the larding to crisp and the bird to brown. Meanwhile fry in the butter the remaining two shallots and truffles (or substitute) minced; add the flour and brown it, then add the water and herbs; simmer the whole for fifteen minutes. After dishing the pheasant, pour away the surplus fat from dripping tin, add the drippings to the gravy, add also the seasoning, lemon-juice and wine, re-heat without boiling, pass through a fine strainer, pour a little over the bird and serve the remainder in a tureen.

FROM THE STREAMS AND POOLS

Collared Trout

Watercress Butter

Stewed Eels

THROUGHOUT the Forest there are numerous streams, mostly rippling over gravel beds, the water often stained brown from the peat. In winter-time when there has been heavy rain they swell to the depth of several feet carrying away overhanging branches. In summer they are reduced to a trickle often drying up completely in places, leaving water only in the deep pools. It is in these pools that the little brown trout become stranded. Being thus restricted they grow to a fair size before the winter rains return to fill the streams again.

The trout being trapped in these pools became easy prey to any stalking gypsy boys with their gift of tickling a trout to catch it. The peasant also would not have had much difficulty in netting the fish to provide himself with a tasty morsel for his tea.

COLLARED TROUT

Wash, clean and dry the fish, split them down the back and remove the bone; dust them with *pepper, salt and mace;* roll up tightly, place them in a dish with *two or three bay leaves,* pour over them *half a pint of vinegar, half a pint of warm water, cover with buttered paper* and bake in a cool oven for three quarters of an hour.

———————

As these small peat stained streams reach the Forest villages they are often added to by natural spring water. This was once the case of the stream that runs through Merry Thought Wood. In the middle of the wood there were wild natural watercress beds freshened by cold spring water. It was here that the gypsies would come to gather and fill their baskets with the green-leafed cress which later they would tie into bunches and sell from door to door together with rabbits and other Forest produce.

WATERCRESS

Wash in three changes of cold water, drain well, and dry. Serve in glass dish, with salt.

WATERCRESS BUTTER

Beat *half a pound of butter* to a cream, then gradually beat in half *a cup of minced watercress,* and *half a tablespoon of lemon juice.* Serve with cold meat sandwiches, or spread on new bread.

T HE western side of the forest is fringed by the river Avon which in places forms its boundary. Here and there the river is fed by some of the Forest streams which form quiet backwaters for breeding fish and eels. The eels found in the river Avon are of an unusual type locally called 'sniggle'. This eel unlike the common eel is slimmer, and its upper jaw is longer. The sniggle eels feeding habits differ from its common cousin; it prefers to feed and move around by day, whereas the ordinary eel is nocturnal in its habits.

It was probably sniggle eels that were caught in the traps as the water passed through the mills beside the River Avon. These eels would have been used as part payment of the rent for the mills as was then the custom to do. Any eels left over would almost certainly have been cooked by the miller's wife using this old Forest recipe.

STEWED EELS

One and a half pounds of eels, one bay-leaf, bunch of sweet herbs, bunch of parsley, one teaspoon of anchovy essence, one onion, half a pint of water, one ounce of butter, one ounce of flour, one tablespoon of vinegar, salt and pepper.

Skin and clean the eels*, cut into pieces two and a half inches long. Make butter hot, fry in it the onion, sliced, also the flour, until browned; add water, then the remaining ingredients. Stew gently, until tender (about 45 minutes). Lift out eels when cooked, and dish, straining sauce over. *A glass of port wine* may be added to the sauce if liked.

*Your fishmonger may do this for you.

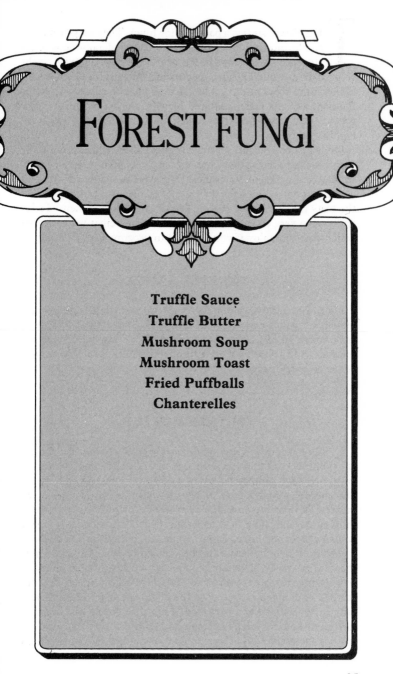

FOREST FUNGI

Truffle Sauce
Truffle Butter
Mushroom Soup
Mushroom Toast
Fried Puffballs
Chanterelles

THE New Forest is a paradise for fungi. They range from the edible mushroom to the highly coloured poisonous toadstools. In the oak and beech woods the puffballs with bright green skins are found in autumn growing amongst the fallen leaves. Beneath the bracken the golden chanterelle and colourful boletus flourish, also the violet-coloured blewits, a great favourite of the gypsies. Of course, they know which fungi are edible and which are highly dangerous.

Once a subterranean species of fungi called truffles were to be found in the Forest. They were hunted for by scent using specially trained dogs and sometimes pigs. Dogs were probably a better idea as the pigs had a liking for the taste of truffles and would often eat the tasty morsels before the pig keeper could rescue them! Today truffles are very expensive but I include two recipes using truffles which you will enjoy if you are able to procure some.

TRUFFLE SAUCE

Clean and peel *four truffles,* and cut them into squares of a quarter of an inch each way. Put them into a sauce with *half a pint of good brown sauce**, and stir over a gentle fire (low burner) for ten minutes. Add a *glassful of sherry,* and if it is liked, *a tablespoonful of lemon juice* and serve.

*Brown Sauce. See Page 28

TRUFFLE BUTTER

Cut up a *pound of butter,* and dissolve it slowly over a clear fire (slow burner); take off the scum which will gather thickly upon it, and when it has simmered for three or four minutes, take it from the fire and let it stand until the buttermilk has settled; pour the buttermilk upon *six ounces of ready-pared truffles,* cut into small thick slices, and laid into a clean saucepan; add seasoning of *freshly pounded mace and fine cayenne, a small saltspoonful of salt, and half a nutmeg.* When the butter has become quite cool, proceed to heat the truffles slowly, shaking the saucepan briskly around, and stew them gently for twenty minutes. Lift them with a spoon into dry earthen or china pans, and pour the butter on them; add sufficient only to cover them and exclude the air. The butter will be finely flavoured and may be used compounding savoury sauces. The truffles themselves will remain good for months if kept free from damp.

The small Forest mushrooms are the button type, their caps being scaley and brownish, quite delicious to eat in their raw state when freshly picked.

MUSHROOM SOUP

Take *one pound of freshly picked mushrooms* and skin them, *slice one small onion, heat a little butter* and fry in it the mushrooms and the onion for three or four minutes, lift out about one dozen of the smallest mushrooms and set aside. Add *three pints of water* to the mushrooms and the onion in the pan, season, boil for half an hour or until the mushrooms are quite soft; pour the soup through a fine sieve and rub through the pulp; put back into the pan, add the dozen small mushrooms, *one ounce of flour mixed with one ounce of butter* into a ball, boil gently for five minutes and pour into a tureen in which *quarter of a pint of cream* has been placed, and serve.

MUSHROOM TOAST

Another way of cooking mushrooms is on toast before a fire, when a lump of butter should be placed on a mushroom and a tumbler put over it. The steam that rises condenses on the side of the tumbler and trickles down on the toast soaking into it and imparting to it the flavour of the mushrooms.

FRIED PUFFBALLS

Gather some *fresh puffballs* and dip them in *egg and breadcrumbs* then fry *with bacon* in the bacon fat. (If the puffballs are large, they may be sliced before coating).

Chanterelle is a fungus reflecting the delicate golden colours of autumn. Trumpet-like with waved edges, possessing the fragrance and taste of apricots, it is usually found growing at the foot of fir trees or beneath the shade of canopies of russet bracken. To our delight this colourful fungus grows on the bank in the lane outside our Abbots Well garden. This is a high bank wooded by slender young birch trees, where if the summer has been warm many colourful fungi appear in the autumn. These range from the very decorative but poisonous fly agaric, their scarlet buttons opening out to parasol shape and spotted white, to the beautiful chanterelle. These usually grow above the wells so that when we go to collect them we take an earthen-ware jug with us to dip out the clear water which we boil the chanterelle in.

CHANTERELLES

Delicious to eat if placed in boiling salted water, and then boiled rapidly for a few minutes. Serve on buttered toast.

THE FARMSTEADS

Bubble and Squeak
Boiled Beef with Vegetables and Dumplings
Pork Sausages
Roast Pork with Apples
Boiled Bacon and Cabbage
Marrow Brandy
Breakfast Eggs
Roasted Capon with Mushrooms
Hampshire Pudding
Syllabub

T HE Forest farms were quite small, and stock consisted mainly of pigs, cattle, chickens and bantams. The farm-houses were often old thatched cottages with the pigsties and cattle byres attached.

The peasant usually kept a small herd of cattle that would graze on the Forest for the best part of the year and eventually provide him with a supply of beef, most of which he salted down and stored for use during the long hard months of winter.

This salted beef was utilized in many ways. For supper it was eaten cold with pickle. Any slices left over were fried with cooked vegetables and eaten for breakfast the next morning.

BUBBLE AND SQUEAK

Cut up some slices of cold boiled salt beef, and fry together with any left-over vegetables and potatoes until lightly browned. Form ingredients into cakes when frying, season with pepper and salt.

BOILED BEEF
WITH VEGETABLES AND DUMPLINGS

Put a *piece of beef* into a pot and *cover with water,* bring to the boil; remove the scum as it rises to the surface, allow meat to simmer for an hour, then add *sliced parsnips and carrots* and boil for a further hour. Dumplings* may be added and cooked with the beef. Season with pepper and salt.

*DUMPLINGS

One teacupful of flour, half a teaspoonful of baking powder, one teaspoonful of chopped suet, half a teaspoonful of salt, water or milk to mix.

Put all the dry ingredients into a basin, mix them well and form into a dough with water or milk. Form into small balls, using a little flour, and drop into the stew.

THE pigs were kept in sties near the farmhouse or in a small compound surrounded by high earth hedges. Every autumn the pigs were turned on to the Forest to feed on fallen acorns and beechmast, as indeed they still are today, this being known as pannage. As their diet consisted entirely of nuts the ham assumed a pleasant flavour found only in the pigs of the New Forest.

Pig killing was always an event. As every part of the pig was made use of everyone got a share. One forester I know remembers how he used to take pig's ear sandwiches for his lunch when he went 'up in Forest' tree cutting.

The farmer's wife made sausages and these were fried with slices of brawn for breakfast.

PORK SAUSAGES

Take about a pound of pork of equal lean and fat meat. Chop up, and add a few *finely chopped sage and thyme leaves, pepper and salt.* Lightly beat *two eggs* and add to the mixture making sure the whole is chopped finely. Sprinkle *flour* onto a board and roll sausages into shape. Fry in the ordinary way.

ROAST PORK WITH APPLES

Take *a leg of pork;* score the skin with the point of a sharp knife (or ask your butcher to do this), rub with *salad oil,* then sprinkle with *salt and pepper.* Put joint of pork into a baking-dish, together with *peeled potatoes* and *a few apples.* Place the dish in the oven and bake at a moderate heat for two hours.

BOILED BACON AND CABBAGE

Bring *a pound of bacon* to the boil in a large saucepan, skim well; put in *a small, well-washed chopped cabbage, two good sized chopped carrots* and *a small chopped parsnip.* Boil gently for about an hour and a half, then add *a few peeled potatoes.* Allow to simmer another half an hour, remove bacon and place on a serving dish surrounded by the vegetables.

The chimney corners of these farmhouses were used for storing other items needing to be kept away from dampness. Rennet was one of these; rennet being the inner stomach of the calf, was usually prepared for use by butchers then returned to the farmhouse where it was salted and stretched out to dry on wooden splinters, or skewers. It was protected from dust and smoke by covering with a paper bag, then pieces were cut off as needed. Perhaps in the opposite corner there would be a large marrow hanging in a net with a jug beneath. This marrow filled with brown sugar would eventually drip delicious marrow syrup into the jug.

MARROW BRANDY

Cut the top off *a large marrow*, and with a long spoon scoop out the centre pulp, *fill with brown sugar;* now add *a little gin* (a miniature bottle is ideal), replace the top and fasten securely with tape or string. Hang up the marrow in a net, place a large jug beneath to catch the liquid that will drip from it after a while. (You may have to pierce it with a skewer). When the jug is full add *a teaspoon of ginger,* bottle up and leave for about three months to mellow.

Outside the farmhouse there were always a few bantams and chickens running around, providing eggs for the family and the occasional bird for the table.

BREAKFAST EGGS

Butter thickly half a dozen small moulds, mix *two tablespoons of minced parsley, and two tablespoons of cooked ham,* and shake into each mould, so that the sides may be covered by the mixture, and reject the surplus. Break *one egg* into each mould, sprinkle with *salt and pepper*; stand in a pan containing water, allowing the water to come within half an inch of the top; simmer slowly till the eggs are just set, then take out the moulds from the pan. Toast some bread and cut into rounds a little larger than the moulds, butter them, and turn out the eggs, one on each piece of toast, and serve.

For a special occasion a capon would be cooked and stuffed with truffles, chestnuts or mushrooms. The following old recipe dates from the days when truffles were plentiful but you can follow it substituting mushrooms.

ROASTED CAPON
WITH TRUFFLES (OR MUSHROOMS)

Clean, wash, and peel some *truffles (or half a pound of mushrooms)*, and cut them into slices about a quarter of an inch thick, fry them in *butter*, and *season with pepper and salt*, and *a little nutmeg*. Place the truffle (mushroom) stuffing inside *the capon*, cover with buttered paper and roast it before a clear fire (in a moderate oven). This dish is usually served without a sauce, but if liked a little may be sent to the table with it, made of good *melted butter*, flavoured with *a quarter of a pound of truffle chips* saved from the peelings *(a few chopped mushrooms)*, and pounded into a mortar with *half an ounce of butter*, and pressed through a sieve.

Any surplus eggs would probably have been made into this delicious pudding.

HAMPSHIRE PUDDING

Line the edge of a pie-dish with *a good puff pastry*. Spread *some jam* at the bottom of the dish, about an inch thick. Beat *the yolks of three, and whites of two eggs*, thoroughly, and add to *three ounces of loaf sugar*, pounded and sifted and *three ounces of dissolved butter*. Beat these together until they are quite thick, pour the mixture over the jam, and bake in a moderate oven until pastry is cooked.

SOMETIMES a few cows would be kept for milking which provided the farmer's wife with cream and enabled her to make her own cheese. In the New Forest the cream cheese was often flavoured with bay leaves which imparted a distinctive flavour when pressed into the cheese. A specialty, as we might expect, was truffle cheese, the truffles being chopped very finely before being added to the cheese.

For festive occasions the farmer's wife would make a drink dating from medieval times called Syllabub. Sweetened and spiced cider was put into a bowl and placed under the cow. She then milked the cow into the bowl which caused the mixture to froth up. In later years the cider was replaced by wine and spirits. I have a recipe for Syllabub dated 1865 which says: 'Put half a pound of sugar into a large bowl together with the juice of two lemons, two large wine-glasses of sherry, one wine-glass of port wine, and one wine-glass of brandy, grate in a little nutmeg, place the bowl under the cow, and milk it full.' Here is a recipe for Syllabub, just as old, but easier for the modern cook to follow!

WHIPPED SYLLABUB (1865)

Weigh *three and a half ounces of fine sugar* and rasp on it the *rinds of a fresh lemon* of good size, then pound or roll it to powder, and put it into a bowl with the *strained juice of the lemon, a large glass of sherry, and one of brandy;* when the sugar is dissolved *add half a pint of very fresh cream,* and whisk the mixture well; take off the froth as it rises, and put it into glasses. These syllabubs should always be made if possible, four-and-twenty hours before they are wanted for table.

COTTAGE GARDENS

Apple Tart
Rhubarb Pie
Blackcurrant Jam
Raspberry Cream Jelly
Woodgreen Cherry Jam
Wild Plum Jam
Evelyn's Bramble Jelly
Strawberry Jam • Strawberry Vinegar
Vegetable Pie
Stuffed Onions • Onion Soup
Spinach
Beetroot Soup
Preserved Mint
Mint Vinegar
Mint Jelly
Candied Mint Leaves

IT appears to have been the tradition in the New Forest for a cottage to have a yew tree near the gate, and a bay tree at the door. Both trees were believed to keep away evil. A yew tree still stands beside what was once the gateway to our old cabin. More evidence of this superstition can be seen in various parts of the Forest where cottages once stood but have now fallen into ruin and disappeared, leaving behind them the remains of their original gardens. I have found three of these abandoned gardens each with its yew tree. In addition, one had only blackcurrant bushes remaining (blackcurrants do well in the Forest), the second had a small orchard of old twisted apple trees, but the third was the wildest and most interesting of them all. It was situated in the deep Forest on the edge of a fir plantation; its yew tree had grown to rival the tall spruce and its bay tree had branched out in all directions mingling with lilac to form a canopy overhead. An ancient Bramley apple tree had grown so high the wind had caught it and bent it almost to the ground, lifting the roots halfway out of the earth. It still leafed and bore its delicious fruit now within easy reach of the browsing deer and other Forest animals.

This old tree was typical of those to be found in most cottage gardens. Unlike today's carefully staked and pruned trees these old fruit trees were left to grow unhindered. Their trunks were leaning and twisted and their boughs bent from supporting crops of fruit on unpruned branches which sometimes almost touched the ground. How juicy and delicious is the fruit from these old-fashioned brands of apples, untouched by sprays and modern methods of gardening! I have four of these old trees in my Forest orchard. The Gascoyne's Scarlet is a brilliant sight in the Autumn, bedecked all over with glowing fruit. Another tree is a mystery to everyone. It is so old that when Juliette de Baïracli Levy sent a sample of its leaves and fruit to be identified by experts it baffled them! The apples have a rough skin tinged with red and Juliette christened it 'Tawny Gypsy'. I also have an old-type russet and a Newton Wonder, a versatile apple that stores well and can be used for cooking as well as dessert.

APPLE TART

A pound and a quarter of apples weighed after they are pared, sliced and cored, will be sufficient for a small tart, and four ounces more for one of moderate size. Lay *a border of pastry* round the dish, just dip the apples into water, arrange them compactly in it, higher in the centre than at the sides, and strew amongst them from *three to four ounces of pounded sugar*, or more should they be very acid: the *grated rind and strained juice of half a lemon* will much improve the flavour. Lay on the cover rolled thin. Place the tart in a moderate oven for half an hour. This may be converted into an *old-fashioned creamed apple tart* by cutting out the cover whilst it is still hot, leaving only about an inch-wide border of pastry round the edge, and pouring over the apples when they have become cold *some well drained cream* piled high and lightly over the fruit.

No cottage garden would be complete without its crown of rhubarb. We discovered some still growing beneath an upturned bucket in the field beyond our garden, once a vegetable patch belonging to an old forester, but now overgrown and neglected.

RHUBARB PIE

Peel the *rhubarb*, and if it is very large divide it into two or three strips, and then into short lengths. Fill the dish as full as it will hold, *sprinkle some sugar* over it, and if liked mix with the fruit a flavouring of *grated lemon-peel and ground ginger, or a little nutmeg grated*. Line the edges of the dish with pastry, moisten these with water, and lay a cover of pastry over all. Press the edges close together and ornament them, then *sprinkle a spoonful or two of cold water* over the pie and dredge *a little white sugar* upon it; bake the pie in a moderate oven until the pastry loosens from the dish, about twenty minutes to half an hour. Serve hot or cold.

BLACKCURRANT JAM

To *one pound of currants allow one pound of sugar* and a *quarter of a pint of water*.

String the currants and wash them, put them in a preserving pan with the water and simmer gently until the fruit is tender. Stir in the sugar and allow to stand for fifteen minutes while the sugar melts. Bring to the boil, then boil moderately fast, stirring all the time, until a little of the jam tested on a cold saucer will set with a wrinkled skin when pushed with a spoon.

———————

Raspberry canes also had their place beside the currant bushes; their sweet fruit providing the ingredients for jam and jelly. For this dish I always use an old china jelly mould, once belonging to my grandmother, now one of my treasures.

RASPBERRY CREAM JELLY

Soak *three quarters of an ounce of gelatine in one pint of water,* add *a pound of raspberries* and *six ounces of sugar.*

Simmer gently for a short while; turn all into a muslin lined sieve and press well as you strain the syrup; set aside to cool. When jelly is just forming, whisk *a quarter of a pint of cream* stiff, gradually add raspberry jelly, beating it in well until smooth, pour into a mould and leave to set.

———————

Woodgreen, a small village in the north west corner of the Forest, was once famed for its black cherry orchards. When the fruit was ripening bells were hung on the trees to frighten off the birds; these became known as the cherry bells of Woodgreen. When the fruit was ready for picking the villagers celebrated by holding 'Cherry Fairs'. You can use a dark cherry to make their jam.

WOODGREEN CHERRY JAM

Stalk and stone *twelve and a half pounds of cherries.* Place in preserving pan with *one pint of currant juice* and *eight pounds of sugar.* Stir well. Cook for half an hour, stirring all the time. Remove from the heat and pour into hot jars. When quite cold, cover with waxed papers *dipped in brandy* then with strong paper covers. Store in a cool place.

WILD cherry trees still grow profusely in the Forest around Woodgreen and in the month of April they are decked in a delicate white blossom with petals so frail they float away on the slightest breeze. Unfortunately, their fruit is too bitter to be pleasant to eat but Juliette de Baïracli Levy used to add a few of these cherries to her blackberry jam to help it set well.

With wild plums it is a different story! They grow well in my Abbots Well garden beside the front gate and overhanging the back porch. Their small yellow plums are sweet when ripe and make a pleasing jam.

WILD PLUM JAM

To *one pound of plums allow one pound of sugar,* and just enough water to cover the bottom of the saucepan. Wash and drain the fruit. Cook until pulped, lift out the stones and drain back all the juice then add sugar and dissolve thoroughly. Bring to the boil again, and boil briskly until set. Stir for a few minutes after removing pan from the stove. Pot up and seal immediately.

The stones from the fruit may be put into muslin, securely fastened and cooked in the preserving pan for added flavour.

––––––––––

Most cottage gardens are invaded in some form by wild vegetation of the Forest. The hedges surrounding our own garden are entwined with brambles but this is to our advantage in the late summer when we are able to pick the clusters of juicy sweet berries. My mother loved to make jams and jellies, and this is one of her favourite recipes.

EVELYN'S BRAMBLE JELLY

Two pounds of blackberries and *a quarter of a pint of water.*
Pick the berries over and remove any stalks. Put them into a preserving pan with the water and bring to the boil; then simmer until the fruit is soft. Strain through a piece of muslin. Put liquid back into saucepan, add sugar allowing *one pound of sugar* to one pint of liquid, stir until dissolved, then boil briskly until set.

My mother never removed her jam from the jars to serve as she said the flavour was lost when exposed to the air for too long. Instead she stood the jar on an attractive saucer, patterned with moss roses or bold nasturtiums, reminiscent of cottage gardens. I treasure her favourite, decorated with a spray of blackberries.

STRAWBERRIES have always been grown in the Forest villages. The meadow beyond our garden was once a strawberry field, an old photograph still exists showing the pickers at work. A forester neighbour remembers how many years ago he would take his strawberries to sell in Southampton returning by moonlight asleep in the bottom of his cart leaving the horse to bring him and his bag of sovereigns safely home.

Today there are still strawberry fields in the Forest and many people now pick their own. The old saying is still true that the air that blows over the Forest smells of strawberries and honey.

STRAWBERRY JAM

Hull *one pound of strawberries,* and crush slightly. Place fruit in a pan over gentle heat; crush with back of wooden spoon. Stir occasionally when coming to the boil, constantly when boiling, add *fourteen ounces of warmed sugar.* Boil about twenty minutes. Allow to cool for fifteen minutes before potting up.

Somewhere on the shelf of a cottager's store cupboard amongst the preserves and cordials you would be certain to find a fruit vinegar. These vinegars were invaluable during the winter months to sooth a sore throat and give relief to a heavy cold. They also provided a refreshing drink on a hot summer day.

STRAWBERRY VINEGAR

Take the stalks from the fruit, which should be of a highly flavoured sort, quite ripe, fresh from the beds, and gathered in dry weather; weigh and put into glass jars, or wide necked bottles, and *to each pound pour one and a half pints of pale white wine vinegar.*

Tie a thick paper over them and let the strawberries remain for three or four days; then pour off the vinegar and empty them into a jelly bag, or suspend them in a cloth, that all the liquid may drop from them without pressure; *replace them with an equal weight of fresh fruit,* pour *the vinegar* upon it and three days afterwards repeat the same process, diminishing a little the proportion of strawberries, of which the flavour ought ultimately to overpower that of the vinegar. In two to four days drain off the liquid very closely, and after having strained it through a linen bag, weigh it and mix with it *an equal quantity of highly refined sugar roughly powdered.* When it is nearly dissolved, stir the syrup over a very clear fire (moderate burner) until it has boiled for five minutes, and skim it thoroughly; pour it into a clean stone pitcher, or into large china jugs, throw a thick-folded cloth over and let it remain till the morrow. Put it into pint bottles, and cork down lightly; after five days they may be closely corked, and stored in a cool dry place.

Damp destroys the colour and injures the flavour of these fine fruit vinegars, of which one spoonful or two in a glass of water affords so agreeable a summer beverage, or in many cases of illness is so acceptable to invalids.

Every cottage garden included vegetables and when meat was not available the cottager would make a vegetable pie which also included mushrooms gathered from the Forest.

VEGETABLE PIE

Cut up *two pounds of potatoes,* put a layer in a pie dish, sprinkle over *a little seasoning,* then *a layer of onion, sliced, the mushrooms, peeled, and more seasoning,* continuing this until the dish is heaped full. Add *two tablespoonfuls of vegetable stock* to the pie. Roll out *a small amount of pastry* and cover the dish, make three holes to ventilate the pie, bake one and a half hours in a moderate oven, add *a little more vegetable stock* and serve.

On cold winter nights supper was usually eaten either around a log fire or before a peat stove so something easy to handle but substantial was needed.

STUFFED ONIONS

Take *three moderate size onions.* Peel and trim them neatly, but be careful not to cut off too much of the tops, for fear the onion may fall to pieces. Scoop out the hearts of the onions, chop them finely, and mix with them *four ounces of lean beef or pork and one ounce of fat bacon (chopped small), a tablespoonful of chopped parsley, three tablespoonfuls of breadcrumbs, two ounces of butter, a little salt and cayenne, and the yolk of an egg* well beaten. Stuff the onion with the meat, and put them into a saucepan side by side, and with them *half a pint of good gravy, and two apples, pared, cored, and chopped small.* Stew the onions until they are perfectly tender, and turn them over once or twice, so that they may be thoroughly cooked right through. Thicken the sauce with *a little flour and butter add pepper and salt,* and serve the onions on a hot dish with the gravy poured around them.

ONION SOUP

Heat *two ounces of butter* in a saucepan and fry in it *three large sliced onions* until brown, add one ounce of flour and brown this also; then add *two quarts of water, salt, half a teaspoonful of peppercorns, one teaspoonful sugar, a bay-leaf and a bunch of parsley,* boil for three quarters of an hour, pour through a fine sieve and rub through the pulp. Beat up the *yolks of two eggs* and place them in a tureen. Boil up the soup and pour it over the yolks, stirring well. Serve with slices of toast.

In a cottage vegetable garden near Abbots Well spinach is still being grown today where once it flourished and was washed clean in the abundant spring water from the well.

SPINACH

Pick *the spinach* leaf by leaf from the stems, and wash it thoroughly, then drain it on a large sieve. Throw it into sufficient *well-salted boiling water* to allow it to float freely, and keep it pressed down with a skimmer that it may be equally done. When quite young it will be tender in from eight to ten minutes. Drain, then press the moisture from it between two trenchers; chop it small, put it into a clean saucepan, with *a slice of fresh butter,* and stir in the whole until well mixed and very hot. Dish and serve immediately. Fried sippets of bread may be served with this vegetable.

BEETROOT SOUP

Put *half a pound of lean shredded veal* into a pan with *an onion, a carrot, a small piece of turnip sliced, a bunch of sweet herbs, a stalk of celery and half a teaspoon of peppercorns,* and simmer slowly *in a quart of water* for one hour; strain. Melt *an ounce of butter* in a saucepan, stir in to it *an ounce of flour* till smooth, add the stock, a large beetroot skinned and sliced thinly, *season with a little salt,* simmer slowly for half an hour pass through a hair sieve, rubbing through the beet. Re-heat, put *quarter of a pint of cream* in to a tureen and pour on the soup.

HERBS played an important part in the cottager's cooking. Of course, the bay leaf was perhaps the most popular but a variety of other herbs were also extensively used. Still growing in my garden is the rosemary bush planted by Juliette de Baïracli Levy. This delightful herb with its starry blue flowers was used for its fragrance in the linen cupboard as well as for its flavour in the kitchen. Enhance the flavour of roast lamb by rubbing olive oil into the meat, season, and place sprigs of rosemary on top.

The most versatile of all herbs is mint. As well as being used in the well-known ways to make a sauce for roast lamb, added to a saucepan of new potatoes and with peas it can be preserved in vinegar and placed in the store cupboard for use during the winter months.

PRESERVED MINT

Wash, dry, and chop *half a pound of freshly picked mint leaves,* place them in a wide necked jar. Put *one pound of sugar* and *one pint of vinegar* into a saucepan, stir with a wooden spoon until sugar is dissolved and allow to come just to the boil, leave until cold. Pour over the chopped mint and seal the jar.

To prepare the sauce for the table, take out required mint and a little liquid and to this add *a little fresh vinegar.*

If all that was needed was the flavour, then a sprig of mint was added to the vinegar and left to infuse.

MINT VINEGAR

Tip *one pint of white wine vinegar* into a saucepan and bring to the boil. Wash *three sprigs of mint,* and squeeze gently between the fingers, and add to the vinegar. Bring to the boil and remove at once from the heat. Cover and leave until cold. Wash *two fresh sprigs of mint* and put into a pint vinegar bottle, and *half a teaspoonful of sugar;* strain the mint vinegar and pour into the bottle. Screw down and store for three months.

Fresh mint added to green apples made a delicious jelly that was served with cold lamb.

MINT JELLY

Wash *three pounds of green apples,* and a *bunch of fresh mint.* Then core and slice the apples, put into a pan *with a few sprigs of the mint;* add *the juice of two lemons* with enough *water* to cover. Simmer until reduced to pulp, strain through muslin, and measure before returning to pan, *add sugar, one pound for each pint of juice,* stir until dissolved. Boil for five minutes. Strip the rest of the *mint leaves* from the stalks and chop them finely, then add them to the liquid. Boil until setting point is reached. Cool slightly, skim jelly, then pour into warm jars. Cover with waxed papers, when quite cool seal down.

At one time as well as making the cake the decorations too were home made. Small flowers such as primroses and violets were candied, the mint leaves were treated this way also to provide leaves for the flowers.

CANDIED MINT LEAVES

Pick *fairly large unblemished mint leaves* with their small stalks on. Spread each thickly with *stiffly whipped egg white,* scatter liberally *with granulated sugar.* Lay on baking sheets and dry out in the oven, bottom shelf, at low temperature, with the door slightly ajar, until absolutely crisp. This takes approximately five hours.

FROM THE HONEY BEE

Raspberries and Honey
Honey Cake
Bog Myrtle Beer
Heather Ale

Abbots Well Mead
Sweet Mead

THERE is an old saying in the Forest 'A swarm of bees in May is worth a load of hay'.

Bee keeping has always been a tradition in the Forest, possibly made so by the constant flow of nectar that is available from early spring to late summer. Amongst the first blossoms that the bees visit is that of the numerous holly trees that grow throughout the Forest. It is said that some of the early honey has an unpleasant flavour when the nectar has been taken from the blossom of the oak trees. The longer season in the Forest is due to the late blooming of the heather and this is when the honey is at its best, so thick, the comb has to be crushed to extract it. It is not only to the forester that this crop is available as many hives from all over the country are brought into the Forest by special licence and placed amidst the heather for the season.

In Virgil's day bee-hives were believed to be of a tall, peaked, dome shape, and they were made from stitched bark, or wattled osiers. Before hiving a swarm the hive was scoured with crushed balm and honeywort. The present day hives are square in shape and made from wood. The original homes of New Forest bees were round skeps made from reeds and straw by the gypsies as they sat around their camp-fires. These skeps were to be found in most cottage gardens providing a supply of honey for the table and for making the old drink of mead.

There are numerous colonies of wild bees in the Forest that live in the hollow trees. They probably originate from swarms leaving hives in the foresters' gardens, and are most likely to be a strain known as New Forest blacks which are said to be bad tempered.

In former days the keepers were allowed to take wild honey from the Forest, but today probably the first to find any that is close to the ground will be the badgers who love honey and have no fear of bees!

When we first moved to Abbots Well the meadow beyond the garden was a wild place. The damp ground produced an abundance of wild flowers, kingcups, water flags, marsh orchids, meadow sweet, lady's bedstraw, cuckoo flowers, and tall rushes. There were mossy banks overhung by willow trees where wild daffodils nodded in the spring.

Growing in one corner of the field were three or four old apple trees, their unpruned branches bending to the ground. It was under these trees that a local bee-keeper kept several hives, the bees from which frequented our garden and kept the fruit trees pollinated, resulting in good crops of fruit. The hives had to be moved when the field was 'cultivated' resulting in a big drop in the number of bees visiting the garden, which in turn affected the fruit. Happily now we have restored the bees to Abbots Well by having our own hives in the garden.

Situated under a bower of entwined honeysuckle and bramble the bees have only to fly over the hedge to reach the heather that covers the hillside beyond the garden.

This recipe originated from the cabin. The honey used was taken from the skeps that stood in the long grass outside the door. The raspberries were picked at Fryer Court and brought to the cabin by Dorelia John, wife of Augustus John, the painter.

RASPBERRIES AND HONEY

Fill a bowl with raspberries of a large size. Over these pour a tablespoonful of honey. Do this every day for two or three days and you will have glasses of sweet juice as well as the fruit.

HONEY CAKE

Eight ounces of self-raising flour, one teaspoonful mixed spice, four tablespoonfuls of honey, four ounces of margarine, two eggs, split almonds, and milk.

Mix flour, sugar, and spice together. Put the margarine, honey and a little milk together and warm, add the beaten eggs, and pour into the dry ingredients.

Mix to a soft dough. Put into a shallow square tin lined with grease-proof paper. Brush with milk and scatter the top with the split almonds.

Bake in a moderate oven for about one hour. Cut into small squares.

On the open heathland in the Forest there are numerous bogs. They are easily seen by their brighter green colour compared with the duller greens surrounding them. These bogs are in themselves gardens containing various water plants, such as the bog asphodel adding its miniature golden stars to the green mossy carpet, the waving cotton grass, and the aromatic bog myrtle, whose sweet fragrance hangs heavy on the surrounding air and from which a refreshing beer can be brewed, using honey.

BOG MYRTLE BEER

Gather enough *bog myrtle leaves* to fill a container, taking care to pick only the leaves and press down. Make a syrup of *boiling water and honey, allowing a pound of honey to a gallon of water,* make enough syrup to cover the leaves. Leave to cool then add *an ounce of dry yeast,* cover and leave to stand for twenty four hours, then strain liquor into a cask. At the end of a week bottle off and cork down firmly.

HEATHER ALE

A large pan of heather tips in full bloom, one ounce of ginger, half an ounce of hops. One pound of honey, and one ounce of dry yeast.

Fill a large pan with the flowering tips of heather in full bloom, cover with water and boil for one hour, then strain into a tub, measure the liquor, and for every gallon add an ounce of ginger, half an ounce of hops, and one pound of honey.

Boil all together for twenty minutes, strain again into the tub and leave for twenty four hours. Add the yeast when cool and when the initial fermentation has ceased skim well and bottle off into strong beer bottles. Cork down. It will be ready to drink in three days.

MEAD

THE New Forest was once famed for the Old English mead that was brewed by the forester.

In Anglo Saxon times we read of mead being in common use for everyone. It was served at royal banquets, and in every monastery the monks had an allowance. The main potion of the wayside taverns was mead, although another liquor was brewed —a rather flat ale.

The Anglo Saxon brewed three kinds of mead from his honey. The one known as Pigment was made from pure honey, with the addition of various spices, and a lacing of a type of wine. This mead was probably served in the Forest manor houses on the occasion of a royal visit.

Another kind, presumably drunk by the lords of the manor and their families, was called Morat; a concoction of honey, water, and the juice of mulberries, the trees of which flourished in England at that time.

The common mead was brewed by the forester using the refuse from the skeps. The imperfect combs were boiled up then strained and the liquor would be put into earthen jars until it fermented. This resulted in a very potent brew often leading to drunkenness. A light hearted story is told in the Forest that if a visitor had been unpleasant during his stay he would be given a large drink of mead before his departure in the hope he would fall from his pony before reaching home!

After the Norman Conquest there was a decline in the English honey-brew as the Normans brought wine with them.

We make mead from our own hives in very much the same way as the forester did back in ancient times. Our hives are square and made from wood but still scoured with sweet herbs. We use handfuls of mint and lavender. The water for making the mead we take from the covered well at Abbots Well.

When boiling up wild comb and cappings the water used should be soft (you can use rain water) as this has an effect on the quality of the wax. The wax should rise to the top and when it is cold it can be lifted off in one piece.

ABBOTS WELL MEAD

The mead is made from wild comb taken from the supers, and the cappings, which are cut from the shallow frames before the honey is extracted.

Place the wild comb and cappings in a pan, cover with cold soft water, or rain water, and bring to the boil. Simmer gently until the wax rises to the top. Allow to cool, remove the wax, strain the remaining liquor into a covered vessel. When cool to room temperature stir in one teaspoonful of mead yeast and put in a warm place to ferment. When bubbling has ceased, strain into a cask with airlock and store for a year before bottling off.

SWEET MEAD

Four pounds of heather honey, one gallon of water, half an ounce of mead yeast.

Boil the water and pour over the warmed honey. Leave to cool, when lukewarm add the yeast, and leave in a warm room to ferment. When bubbling has ceased leave to stand in a cool place for a few weeks. Strain into a cask and store for a year before bottling off.

HOME BAKING

Wholemeal Bread

Badger Cottage Girdle Scones

Ham Girdle Cakes

Potato Girdle Cakes

Wholemeal Biscuits

Oatmeal Biscuits

Aunt Addie's Parkin

Uncle Harry's Bread Pudding

Gingerbread Men

Gingernuts

UNTIL quite recently, flour was still being ground in the mills in some New Forest villages. In the past the peasant bought his flour by the sack and baked his own bread. Like our cabin, most Forest cottages had big open fireplaces with wide hearths and baking ovens to one side. It was believed that a brick oven heated with wood was far superior to the iron ovens attached to kitchen ranges, for baking bread. With the iron ovens, the surface of the bread became hardened and brown long before the heat had sufficiently penetrated the centre of the dough. The brick oven was well heated beforehand from within with faggot wood or with a faggot and two or three solid logs. When the wood had burnt clear the fire was raked out and the door was closely shut for half an hour before the baking commenced so the heat was well sustained for bread, pies and cakes.

Here is an old recipe for bread which succeeds as well in a modern oven.

WHOLEMEAL BREAD

One and a half pounds of wholemeal flour, half an ounce of fresh yeast, one and a half teaspoons of salt, one teaspoonful of soft brown sugar, three quarters of a pint of tepid water.

Mix the flour and salt together and make a well in the dough. Cream the yeast and sugar and add tepid water, pour into the well and mix with the flour. Knead thoroughly until it leaves the hands cleanly. Flour the bottom of basin, put the dough to rise in a warm place (the best is a rack above the fireplace), and let it be there for two hours if possible. Knead again, using more flour, send directly to a well heated oven, and bake for one hour.

IN winter, with a log fire in the cabin, we sometimes have girdle scones for tea. A girdle (sometimes called a griddle) is a round piece of thick iron hanging on a chain and heated over an open fire. It can also be used on a range or stove. You can use a grill burner for these recipes or a griddle if you have one. The griddle should be well heated whilst preparing the dough. Before cooking, it can be either greased or sprinkled with flour. Afterwards, the girdle should never be washed. Clean it by rubbing with coarse salt and a piece of paper, then give it a final dust.

Our girdle was given to us by the Forest naturalist, Eric Ashby. It came from 'Badger Cottage' where it was regularly used by his mother to make these delicious scones.

BADGER COTTAGE GIRDLE SCONES

One pound of flour, half a teaspoonful cream of tartar, one teaspoonful carbonate of soda, a little salt, and sour milk.

Sieve all the dry ingredients into a basin and make a well in the centre. Add enough milk to make a light dough, turn out on a floured board, and divide into four. Then take one piece at a time and flatten it into a round scone, about half an inch thick. Cut in four again and place the scones on a hot greased girdle. Cook about five minutes on either side. The scones should be nicely browned on both sides, and they are ready when the edges are dry. Serve with butter.

A few currants may be added if liked.

If we are using the girdle at supper-time we cook ham or potato cakes. Both are very tasty.

HAM GIRDLE CAKES

Sift *three cups of flour, three teaspoons of baking powder,* and *a pinch of salt* into a basin. Add *two cups of milk to a lightly beaten egg.* Stir into the dry ingredients. Beat in *two tablespoons of melted butter and half a cup of minced boiled ham.* Rub the hot girdle over with *a piece of fat bacon* and if the girdle is hot enough the fat should fizzle loudly. Cook mixture in tablespoonfuls, turning cakes when they are brown beneath and full of bubbles on top.

POTATO GIRDLE CAKES

Take some *freshly boiled potatoes* and mash while still hot. *Add salt and a small piece of butter.* Then roll out thinly, using *a little flour,* to prevent the mixture sticking. Cut into rounds, and cook the cakes on a hot greased girdle until brown on both sides. Serve hot spread with butter.

A plain biscuit made from an ancient recipe but so versatile it can be eaten with cheese as a mid-morning snack or spread with honey and eaten equally well for tea.

WHOLEMEAL BISCUITS

Take *one pound of wholemeal flour, one teaspoonful of salt, enough water to make a moderately stiff dough.* The dough must be very well kneaded until it feels elastic. Then roll out, cut and prick, and bake in a moderate oven for about twenty minutes.

There is another old recipe for a sweet oatmeal biscuit which I like to keep in a tin in the kitchen to accompany a cup of tea or coffee for any callers. One of my occasional visitors is an old gypsy lady who comes to collect rags. She admits to being over eighty; her dry wrinkled face full of character is framed by two grey plaits looped and fastened over her ears. I love to listen to her talking about the wild herbs of the Forest and watch as she tips her tea into the sauce with long suntanned fingers before lifting it to her lips to slowly drink the contents.

OATMEAL BISCUITS

Half a pound of medium oatmeal, half a pound of flour, quarter of a pound of margarine, a saltspoonful of salt, two ounces of sugar, a little milk.

Rub margarine into flour lightly. Add all other ingredients. Mix to a stiff paste with milk or water. Roll out, and bake till crisp in a moderate oven.

Ringwood is a bustling little town in the Avon valley, close to the Forest boundary. Every Wednesday is market day. Fruit and vegetable stalls line the main street and there is an undercover livestock market where you can bid for anything from a horse to a rabbit. It is a great gathering place for the gypsies where they meet to buy and sell their horses. I used to combine a visit to the market and tea with my aunt and uncle who lived nearby. Aunt Addie baked the most delicious parkin.

AUNT ADDIE'S PARKIN

Two pounds of treacle, two pounds of medium oatmeal, half an ounce of mixed spice, six ounces of margarine, four ounces of citron or mixed peel.

Melt butter and treacle in a saucepan. Mix dry ingredients together, add to pan and beat well. Cover with a cloth and allow to stand all night. Bake in a well greased tin in a slow oven for one and a half to two hours. This cake must be cold before turning out.

Not only my aunt baked but Uncle Harry also was an excellent cook, his speciality being bread pudding. Every week when I took my leave I was given a freshly baked pudding to bring home. Sadly now they have moved away but I remember the smell of parkin and bread pudding, the noise of the market, and mingled together they make a very happy memory.

UNCLE HARRY'S BREAD PUDDING

Cut *half a pound of stale bread* into small pieces, put into a basin and *cover with milk*. Leave to soak, then squeeze until dry and beat with a fork. Mix with *three ounces of shredded suet, two ounces of demerara sugar, four ounces of dried fruit, and half a teaspoonful of mixed spice. Stir in two eggs.* Press the mixture into a greased sandwich tin and bake for about thirty five minutes in a moderate oven.

In Furzey Gardens, near Minstead, there is an ancient cottage that has been made into a small centre for all the dying crafts of the New Forest. Here one can find gingerbread men for sale made in the old fashioned shapes, the same as they were hundreds of years ago when they were baked in patterned moulds.

GINGERBREAD MEN

Mix *one pound of flour, and three teaspoonfuls of baking powder* thoroughly; melt *quarter of a pound of butter* and mix it with *half a pound of treacle or golden syrup and one ounce of powdered ginger,* and then incorporate the whole of the ingredients, which will form a soft, dark coloured dough. Roll the dough out thinly, cut into shapes, and place on a well greased baking tin, and bake in a cool oven for about twenty minutes.

———————

Michaelmas is the time of year we associate with farms changing hands, roast goose, cottage gardens full of autumn flowers, and of course travelling fairs. In Ringwood every year at carnival time there is a large fair. Apart from the rides and side shows there is an open sided caravan that sells old fashioned sweetmeats, and fairings; home-made nougat, toffee apples, and the traditional gingernuts without which no fair would be complete.

GINGERNUTS

One pound of flour; three teaspoonfuls of baking powder; quarter of a pound of butter; half a pound of treacle or golden syrup, half an ounce of caraway seed; half an ounce of citron or candied lemon peel, and one egg.

Mix the flour and baking powder thoroughly, then add the caraway seed and candied peel cut fine, melt the butter and mix it with the treacle and ginger, then incorporate the two mixtures and add one egg. After working the whole together roll the dough into thin sheets, cut it into circles with rim of a wineglass; place the nuts thus formed on a well greased tin and bake in a cool oven for about twenty minutes or half an hour, according to the thickness of the nuts.

AUTUMN'S HARVEST

Blackberry Jam•Blackberry Wine
Hedgerow Wine
Blackberry Cordial•Blackberry Vinegar
Sloe Jelly•Wild Apple Jelly
Stuffed Marrow•Marrow Jam
Pumpkin Jam•Pumpkin Pie
Cheese and Chestnut filled Potatoes
Green Tomato Chutney
Mixed Pickle•Pickled Onions
Apple Cake•Cider•Apple Wine
Damson Cheesecakes•Damson Jam
Pickled Damsons
Stewed Pears•Medlar Jelly
Autumn Preserve
Hazelnut Chutney•Hazelnut Bread
Chestnut Soup•Chestnut Stuffing

AS summer begins to fade in the Forest and merge into autumn, bringing the early morning mists, fragile spiders' webs studded with dew-drops lace every plant and bush. Mellow days give way to crisp evenings and at night the harvest moon shines brightly over the Forest. This is a colourful time when the whole Forest is ablaze with golds, reds and russets. The cottage gardens are mantled in purple as michaelmas daisies bloom alongside bronze and pink chrysanthemums. This is the time for harvest suppers, and Halloween, bonfires and big moons, and for trying out old and new recipes with the harvest to be gathered from countryside and garden.

The air surrounding the groups of hives placed in the heather during the summer, for the bees to gather the nectar, is heavy with the sweet smell of honey. Chestnuts are scattered on the ground, and under the tall bracken chanterelles are to be found, and everywhere blackberries and sloes are hanging in clusters from the bushes.

The cottage gardens too are full; marrows and pumpkins have grown large. In the orchard the apples and damsons are ready for picking.

This is the season for making jams, jellies, chutneys, and wine, in fact one of the busiest periods in a forester's kitchen.

One of the first of autumn's fruits to be ready for harvesting are blackberries, ripening just when the early fallers are down in the apple orchard. You can combine the two fruits to make a delicious pie.

The original way they made 'Wild Blackberry Pie' in the Forest was to fill an open pastry case with blackberries. Cooked in this way I find the seed too crunchy. I prefer to transfer the flavour of the blackberries to the apple by first simmering the berries in a little water, crushing them gently as they soften, then strain the liquid onto the prepared apple and simmer until soft with added sugar to taste. This can be eaten as it is with cream or used as filling for a pie.

BLACKBERRY JAM

Six pounds of blackberries, five pounds of sugar, one gill of water per pound of fruit.

Use only sound fruit. Mix in a few unripe berries. Rinse and drain.

Cook fruit and water together by simmering only until juice begins to run. Raise the heat and cook until fruit is quite tender.

Pour in the sugar, stir until dissolved, boil rapidly, then test. Cover jars while hot.

The donkeys that roam free love to take ripe clusters of blackberries from the bushes. Often I have been joined by a friendly donkey intent on securing the juiciest berries before me!

Every year we pick blackberries for wine making. The baskets are lined with bracken fronds and we seek out a place away from roads and dusty tracks where the berries are clean as washing them tends to take away the flavour and natural juices.

BLACKBERRY WINE

Eight pounds of blackberries, eight pints of boiling water, two and a half pounds of sugar to each gallon of juice, a quarter of an ounce of dry yeast.

Place the blackberries into a container then pour the boiling water over them, and crush the fruit to extract the juice. Leave standing for four days to infuse. Strain the liquid off. Measure the juice and add sugar and yeast.

Leave in a warm place to ferment. Skim off at intervals, and after bubbling has ceased, siphon off, or strain through thick muslin into a cask, filling the cask completely. Cork and leave at least three months. Pour into bottles, cork, and leave to mature.

The bramble wines are very good made hot with spices added. They are especially warming to serve around the bonfire on Guy Fawkes night when all around the frost is glittering and the stars shine coldly overhead.

HEDGEROW WINE

One gallon of blackberries, two pounds of sloes, one gallon of boiling water, four ounces of sugar, half an ounce of dry yeast, and a slice of toast.

Pour the boiling water over the fruit, and leave for a week. Mash the fruit with a wooden spoon daily. Strain and squeeze all the liquid from the fruit. Strain the liquid through muslin. Add the sugar and stir until dissolved. Spread the yeast onto the toast and put on the wine and place in a warm room to ferment. After a week skim and bottle. Keep for several months to mature.

The children, too, want a hot blackberry drink but as the wine is too strong a special cordial is brewed and this can also be served hot. It is equally refreshing taken cold on a hot day.

BLACKBERRY CORDIAL

Two pints of blackberry juice, one pound of sugar, one ounce of whole cloves, one ounce of stick cinnamon, one ounce of whole nutmeg.

Tie spices together in a piece of clean muslin, place in blackberry juice and boil for thirty minutes, strain off liquid. Bottle immediately and seal down. Dilute to taste.

Blackberry vinegar is a must in my store cupboard for the winter months, so soothing when taken for a sore throat or heavy cold.

BLACKBERRY VINEGAR

Six pounds of blackberries, eight pints of white wine vinegar, allow *one pound of sugar to one pint of juice.*

Fill glass jars or wide-necked bottles with very ripe but perfectly sound freshly gathered blackberries, freed from their stalks, and cover them with the white wine vinegar: they may be left to infuse from a week to ten days, or the vinegar may be poured from them in four or five days. Strain through muslin, and measure the juice, allowing one pound of sugar to each pint. Bring to the boil and simmer gently for five minutes, then bottle and cork well.

A measure of this is delightful in cold water as a refreshing drink on a hot summer's day or with hot water as a night cap for a cold.

The blackthorn bushes now will be dotted with dark sloes. Too tart to eat in their natural state but very palatable when made into jelly to accompany cold meat.

SLOE JELLY

Prepare *six pounds of sloes* by pricking them with a fork. Put them in a preserving pan with *three pints of water,* simmer until quite tender, then mash well. Strain through a jelly bag, measure juice and return to a clean preserving pan. Bring to the boil, remove from the heat and stir in *one pound of sugar for each pint of juice*. Return to the heat, bring to the boil, stirring. Boil rapidly without stirring until setting point is reached. Skin, then pour jelly into warm clean jars. Cover.

The wild apple trees which in springtime were covered with bright pink blossom now shed their fruit which you can collect to make a tart jelly that is very agreeable with cold pork.

WILD APPLE JELLY

Six pounds of wild apples, three pints of water, root ginger, and sugar. Wash the apples and cut away any bruised parts. Cut into quarters without peeling or coring. Put into a preserving pan with water and ginger, simmer for an hour, or until the fruit is pulped, adding a little more water if necessary. Strain through a jelly bag. Measure juice in pints and return to a clean preserving pan. Bring to the boil, remove from the heat and stir in sugar, allowing *one pound of sugar for every pint of apple juice.* Return to gentle heat, stir till sugar dissolves. Bring to the boil. Boil rapidly to setting point. Remove any scum. Pot and cover.

In the cottage gardens the vegetables are plentiful and the pumpkins and marrows are growing large ready to take their place in the Harvest Festival. Not all the marrows reach maturity and half-grown ones are delicious when stuffed with a tasty filling.

STUFFED MARROW

One large marrow, two tablespoonfuls chopped beef, or mince, two tablespoonfuls of chopped ham, two teaspoonfuls of finely chopped parsley, a little powdered mace, pinch of lemon thyme, pepper, salt and one tablespoonful of tomato ketchup, one egg, four tablespoonfuls of breadcrumbs, white or cheese sauce.

If the marrow is young there is no need to peel it. Wash, and cut marrow in half (widthways); scoop out the seed. Boil the mince for 20 mins. Put all the stuffing ingredients in a basin and blend together with sufficient beaten egg to bind. Fill the marrow with the stuffing, and place the two halves together.

Tie in muslin, and steam until the marrow is completely cooked, about 35 mins. Place in a hot vegetable dish, coat with white or cheese sauce, and serve.

The larger marrows being much riper make an excellent jam.

MARROW JAM

Four pounds of vegetable marrow weighed when it has been peeled and seeded, *three pounds of sugar, finely grated rind and juice of two lemons, one ounce of ground ginger.*

This should not be made until the marrows are ripe and yellow. If made when they are soft and new, the jam and preserve will be watery and will not set or keep well.

Cut the marrow into small chunks, and leave in a bowl for twelve hours then drain off any water there may be, and dry the pieces in a clean cloth. Pour the sugar over the marrow and leave for twenty four hours.

Put it into the preserving pan with the lemon juice and grated rind and simmer for half an hour, bring to the boil and boil gently for another hour when the syrup should be thick and the marrow transparent.

———

Every autumn at 'The Load of Hay' Fordingbridge, a pumpkin show is held. From miles around pumpkins of enormous sizes are brought in to be weighed. Whilst weighing is in progress, (which sometimes takes most of the afternoon), you can look at the childrens' fancy dressed pumpkins competition. They do not have to be large, and are dressed up with hats on, painted faces, feathers, and all manner of decorations to represent various characters and objects. If you wish for a little refreshment before returning to the courtyard to see the winning pumpkin there is a stall selling a sweet liqueur type wine made from the pumpkin and also jars of pumpkin jam.

PUMPKIN JAM

Six pounds of pumpkin, cut into small slices, four pounds of sugar, strained juice of one lemon, and two ounces of ground ginger.

Cut the pumpkin into small pieces, put into a bowl and sprinkle with sugar and lemon juice. Leave for twelve hours. Pour off the syrup liquid into the preserving pan, bring to the boil moderately fast until the syrup is very thick and the pumpkin quite soft.

The ginger may be omitted if the delicate flavour of the pumpkin is preferred.

Some of the pumpkins are afterwards sold to local fruit and vegetable shops where they are cut into wedges and sold for making puddings and jam. I usually make my piece into a pudding.

PUMPKIN PUDDING

Take *a large slice of pumpkin* pare it, and remove the seeds. Cut it into thin slices, and boil these gently in water until they are quite soft, then rub them through a fine sieve with the back of a wooden spoon. Measure the pulp, and with each pint put *four ounces of butter, six ounces of sugar, a little grated nutmeg, and six drops of almond essence, half a teaspoonful of powdered ginger.* Stir the mixture briskly for a minute or two, then add *a third of a pint of hot milk* and *four well-beaten eggs. A glassful of wine or brandy* may be added or not. Pour the pudding into a buttered dish, and bake in a moderate oven for about half an hour.

PUMPKIN PIE

Two pounds of pumpkin cut into small pieces, *two large apples, two tablespoonfuls of seedless raisins or sultanas, three ounces of brown sugar, half a teaspoonful of mixed spice, quarter of a teaspoonful of ground cinnamon, grated rind of one lemon and its strained juice, short crust.*

Cook the pumpkin and the apple separately, until both are soft. Drain the pumpkin thoroughly. Beat the apple to a pulp, but cut the pumpkin into small dice. Mix them together with the sugar, spices, lemon rind and lemon juice. Line a pie dish with short crust, fill with the pumpkin mixture, bake in a fairly hot oven for twenty five to thirty minutes.

Potatoes roasted in their jackets filled with cheese and chestnuts always remind me of Guy Fawkes night when they are eaten around the bonfire with glasses of home made wine. A number of fires are lit in the New Forest villages where sometimes in the glow of the flames a glimpse will be caught of an animal attracted by the warmth, a pig as it forages for acorns, or ponies dreaming perhaps of gypsy campfires they once knew long ago. All too soon the flames become dying embers and the glow fades till the only lights remaining are the stars above or a lantern hanging on a tree ready to light the way home.

CHEESE AND CHESTNUT FILLED POTATOES

Scrub potatoes, prick all over and brush with melted butter. Wrap separately in foil, and bake for one hour towards the top of a moderate oven, turn foil back to form dishes. Slice tops off potatoes, scoop out the flesh into a bowl and mash with *top of milk, butter, and seasoning, add grated cheese and chestnut filling.* Then refill potato jackets and return to the oven to brown for a few minutes.

CHESTNUT FILLING

Prick chestnuts and put into water, bring to the boil and simmer for five minutes. Peel removing all skins, place nuts in a saucepan, *cover with milk,* boil till tender. Strain off surplus milk then mash nuts and add *a pinch of salt and a little sugar.*

At the end of summer there are usually a lot of tomatoes which do not ripen. These can either be pickled or made into chutney.

GREEN TOMATO CHUTNEY

Two pounds of green tomatoes, one large onion thinly sliced, *a tablespoonful of salt, four ounces of seedless raisins* cut small, *six ounces of brown sugar, one teaspoonful of dried mustard, one teaspoonful of ground ginger, pinch of cayenne pepper, three quarters of a pint of vinegar.*

Wash and dry tomatoes and cut into thick slices. Put them in layers in a bowl with sliced onion and salt between, and leave twelve hours. Mix the mustard with the ginger and a little of the tomato liquor, and turn all into a stewpan with the rest of the ingredients. Stir well with a wooden spoon as the chutney heats, and simmer gently until it is soft and thick. Let it cool a little, then pour into wide-mouthed heated glass jars. When chutney is cold, cover, and tie down.

MIXED PICKLE

The following vegetables make a good mixed pickle: *cauliflower, cucumber, green tomatoes, onions, and marrow.*

Prepare the vegetables, with the exception of the marrow, and soak in brine for twenty four hours. Peel the marrow, remove seeds, and cut into small squares, sprinkle with salt, and let stand for twelve hours. Drain the vegetables, rinse, pack into jars, cover with cold spiced vinegar,* tie down, and store for at least one month before eating.

Onions I pickle in relays. The first batch is for Christmas, by this time they will be just ready for eating. The second batch is for use during the summer and are packed into large stone storage jars.

A last minute picnic can be easily assembled with crusty bread, butter, cheese, pickled onions and a bottle of white wine.

PICKLED ONIONS

Choose small onions or shallots. To make the peeling easier, do it under cold water. *Soak in brine* for twenty four hours, then drain and wash well. Pack into jars, using a wooden spoon handle and pour the *cold spiced vinegar** over. Seal and store.

Brine. Allow *two ounces of salt to one pint of water* (sufficient for about one pound of vegetables).

SPICED VINEGAR*

To each quart of vinegar add an ounce of the following spices: cloves, peppercorns, allspice, chillies, blade mace, mustard seed, and root ginger. (Alternatively you can buy them already mixed as "pickling spice").

Bring just to the boil in a covered pan, then remove from the heat, and allow to infuse until the vinegar is flavoured, usually about two hours is sufficient. Strain, and use as required.

APPLE picking time means a week of hard work for my husband and myself if the crop is good. Picking, grading, and carrying the apples to the store can be time consuming and we often work until after dark. Having no electricity in the apple house it all has to be done by moonlight and the dim light of an oil lantern. The blended smells of apples and burning oil is something I shall always connect with crisp autumn evenings.

After the apples are graded the bruised or wormy ones are brought into the kitchen for immediate use. I take this opportunity to use some of these apples to make our favourite cake.

APPLE CAKE

Eight ounces of self-raising flour, four ounces of butter, four ounces of soft brown sugar, half a teaspoonful of cinnamon, half a pound of chopped apples, and two eggs.

Sieve the flour and cinnamon into a mixing bowl and rub in the butter. Add the sugar, apples and eggs. Mix gently to a soft dough, and put it into a greased tin. Bake in a moderate oven for about an hour.

Cider making was once carried out all over the Forest, as most cottages had an orchard attached to their land. In many cases cider presses were kept outside in the orchard. For those not owning their own press an old man used to come around the village with one on a horse and wagon. There is still a cider press in use in our neighbouring village, Blissford, to this day.

CIDER

Let sixty pounds of apples stand in a pile for one to three weeks to soften, then chop them roughly and press through a fruit press. Failing a press, use an old wooden mangle; put the fruit in a strong hessian bag, and pass the open end of the bag through the mangle first. Take care to keep the apples going through evenly, otherwise you might be left at the end with a mass which will not go through the rollers, and the bag will probably burst. Allow the juice to ferment for six weeks, then syphon off into a clean jar. The cider will be ready to drink immediately, if required.

Not having a cider press or the quantity of apples needed for cider making we are quite happy to use our spare apples to make a modest apple wine.

APPLE WINE

Eight pounds of apples (sweet and cooking mixed), six pints of cold boiled water, syrup made from three pounds of sugar and one and a half pints of water.

Windfall apples can be used for this wine. Cut them into pieces, cover with cold boiled water and leave to stand for three days; each day squeeze them with your hands and stir. Finally strain off the liquid and add sugar syrup to taste (made by dissolving the sugar in the water and boiling for a minute). Put the mixture into a cask or jar fitted with a fermentation lock, and allow to ferment for about four weeks. Syphon into clean jars and cork securely while it is still fermenting; the wine may be drunk in three weeks' time; if preferred, it may be left to become still and clear — about a month.

No Forest orchard would be complete without one or two damson trees. An orchard near us on the side of a hill has damson trees growing the length of it, their straggling branches overhanging the lane dropping the fruit onto the ground beneath. Every autumn with the farmer's permission we go into the orchard and pick baskets full of this dark fruit with its purplish bloom then take them back to the farm to be weighed.

There is such a variety of things you can do with damsons, but cheesecakes are one of the first things I make when I get home.

DAMSON CHEESECAKES

To make the curd for the filling. *One pint of milk and one pint of sour milk, a teaspoonful of lemon juice and one egg.*

Beat the egg with the sour milk. Put the fresh milk in a saucepan and bring to the boil. Add the egg and sour milk mixture to the boiled fresh milk, add the lemon juice and stir all together until the curds rise to the top. Pour the mixture into a piece of muslin, and allow the curds to strain in this as the whey runs off. When the curds are firm and free from whey they are ready.

Line small patty tins with *a good short pastry* rolled thinly; mix the curds with *two tablespoonfuls of cream, one beaten egg and a pinch of nutmeg.*

Fill the pastry cases with spoonfuls of the mixture; drop *a damson* into each one before baking.

Bake in a fairly hot oven for fifteen to twenty minutes.

DAMSON JAM
Try this with hot scones and cream!

Four pounds of damsons, half a pint of water, three pounds of sugar.

The fruit for this jam should be freshly gathered and quite ripe. Simmer them gently in the water until they are soft. Catch up the stones as they rise to the top. Then stir in the sugar, and when it has dissolved bring to the boil, keeping it stirred and thoroughly skimmed. Boil moderately fast until a little will set when tested.

Pot when very hot and cover when quite cold.

PICKLED DAMSONS
Especially good at Christmas with cold turkey

Three pounds of ripe damsons, two pounds of sugar, four pints of vinegar, one teaspoonful of ground allspice, one teaspoonful of ground ginger, one teaspoonful of ground mace, and one teaspoonful of ground cloves.

Wash and prick the fruit, put into a pan with the sugar, add the spices and vinegar, and cook until tender, but not broken. Drain well and put into jars. Boil the syrup for fifteen minutes, and strain into the jars. The next day pour off the syrup, re-boil and pour over the fruit again. When cold, cover and store for three months before using.

Up the hill from our cottage, overhanging a ditch, stands an old pear tree remaining from the days when a cottage stood there. Each year it sheds its fruit into the ditch beneath where they lie untouched by the Forest animals who do not seem to have the same liking for the pears as they do apples. Gathered up and stored for a few days these pears cook beautifully when they turn a bright pink.

STEWED PEARS

From twelve to eighteen pears; a small lemon; twelve cloves; half a pound of moist sugar; some water.

Peel the pears, cut each in half and remove the core; cut the lemon in thin slices; lay the pears and lemon-peel in layers, in an earthen jar with a cover to it, putting in a clove here and there, and strewing sugar over each layer. Pour in sufficient water to cover the pears completely; set the jar in a cool oven and bake for four or five hours.

In Ringwood, there is a nursery selling some of the old types of fruit trees and shrubs. Tucked away in a corner is an old medlar tree with a twisted trunk. In the autumn it is so laden with fruit the branches hang down over the wall. We decided to buy a young medlar tree for our own garden and planted it on the edge of the wood overhanging the watermeadow. Much to everyone's surprise it bore seven medlars in its first season. The russet foliage of the tree is a delight in the autumn.

MEDLAR JELLY

Three pounds of medlars, sugar, two pints of water, and one lemon.

Cut up the medlars which should be soft, put into a preserving pan and just cover with water, add a whole lemon cut up. Simmer until the fruit is soft. Mash with a wooden spoon and strain through a jelly bag. To every pint of juice, add three quarters of a pound of sugar and stir until dissolved. Boil until setting point is reached, pot up. Seal when cold.

When all the fruit is gathered in what could be nicer than to blend them together to capture all their flavours in one jar!

AUTUMN PRESERVE

One pound of cooking apples, one pound of pears, one pound of damsons, half a pint of water, sugar (three quarters of a pound to a pint of cooked fruit), half a level teaspoon of nutmeg, one ounce of root ginger, one ounce of chopped almonds.

First simmer the damsons in water until tender enough to remove stones. Meanwhile peel, core, and slice apples and pears, place in preserving pan, and add stoned damson puree, cook until fruits are tender. Measure fruit and add sugar accordingly. Add nutmeg and bruised ginger. Stir until sugar has dissolved, boil rapidly until setting point is reached, fifteen to twenty minutes. Skim and remove ginger. Add almonds, pour into warm jars, cover and seal.

In the hedgerows the hazel trees are shedding their nuts. In the woods also the prickly jackets on the tall chestnut trees are bursting and scattering their shiny brown fruit onto the ground. This is the time for nutting, with the help of a walking stick to reach the branches, a pair of strong gloves for protection when opening the prickly husks of the chestnuts, and a basket. The hazelnuts are probably the most difficult to find in any quantity. You have to be very quick to secure them before the squirrels, they seem to know just the right moment to collect their favourite food.

Should you be fortunate enough to gather some of these sweet little nuts then you could add them to more ingredients and make an unusual chutney.

HAZELNUT CHUTNEY

One pound of cooking apples, one pound of prunes, half a pound of hazelnuts, half a pint of wine vinegar, ten ounces of brown sugar, half a teaspoonful of cinnamon, quarter of a teaspoonful of powdered alspice, and a pinch of cayenne pepper.

Pour boiling water over the prunes and leave to soak for twenty four hours. Peel and core the apples, chop finely and stew until tender with a little of the sugar. Chop the nuts finely. Remove the prune stones, and cut the prunes into pieces. Put the vinegar into the pan, add the sugar and mix in the remaining ingredients. Boil all together for an hour, stirring continuously. Pot and cover at once.

Perhaps you would prefer to capture their pleasing flavour in a bread. This you could spread with butter and eat before the fire at tea time.

HAZELNUT BREAD

One and half cups of flour, one teaspoonful of salt, two cups of wheaten meal, half a cup of brown sugar, one large teaspoon of baking soda, one cup of chopped hazelnuts, two cups of milk, and half a cup of treacle.

Sift flour and salt into a basin. Stir in wheaten meal, sugar, and baking soda, the sugar and soda sifted together. Add finely chopped hazelnuts and treacle, or use half treacle and half syrup. Beat for a few moments till light. Bake in a buttered loaf tin for about an hour. This loaf is better kept for a few days before cutting.

Chestnuts are the most versatile of nuts lending themselves to a variety of uses in cooking. The old traditional way of roasting them in the glowing embers is still my favourite way of eating them but here are two recipes you will enjoy.

CREAM OF CHESTNUT SOUP

A pound and a half of chestnuts, two quarts of stock, seasoning of salt, mace, and cayenne, three quarters of a pint of rich cream.

Prepare the chestnuts by slitting the shell of each and boiling in water for about ten minutes. Shell and peel the skins whilst still hot. Stew the chestnuts in a good stock for about three quarters of an hour, or until they break when touched with a fork; drain, and pound them smoothly, mix with them by slow degrees the proper quantity of stock; add sufficient mace, cayenne, salt to season the soup, and stir it often till it boils. Add cream and serve.

And you can make a very good stuffing for the turkey.

CHESTNUT STUFFING

One pound of chestnuts, half a pint of stock, one ounce of butter, grated rind of one lemon, one teaspoonful of sugar, quarter of a pound of bread-crumbs, quarter of a pound of ham or bacon, one dessertspoonful of parsley, one egg and seasoning.

Remove the outside shell from the nuts, then blanch them and remove the inner skin. Stew the nuts in stock or water until they are quite tender and dry. Then pound them to a paste with the ham or bacon finely chopped. Add all the other ingredients, moistening with beaten egg or a little milk.

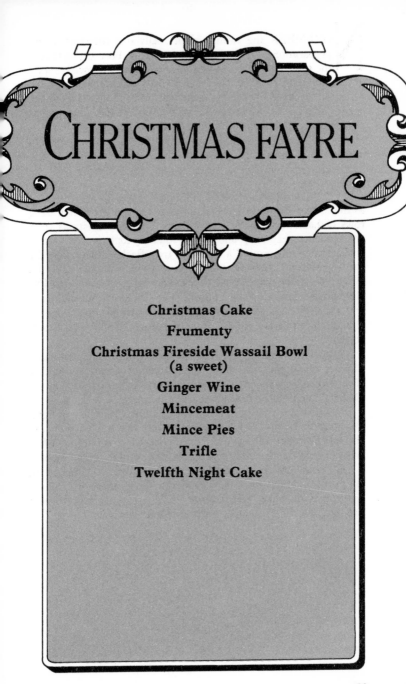

CHRISTMAS FAYRE

Christmas Cake

Frumenty

Christmas Fireside Wassail Bowl
(a sweet)

Ginger Wine

Mincemeat

Mince Pies

Trifle

Twelfth Night Cake

NOVEMBER the twenty-sixth really sees the start of the preparations for Christmas in the New Forest. For that is the traditional date on which the gypsies are allowed to start picking the holly to sell at the local markets and to make wreaths. Already they have filled their sacks with moss gathered from the boggy paths on the side of the hill above Abbots Well. This moss is used in the foundations of the wreaths. One old gypsy lady living in the village can always be seen at that time of year colourfully dressed in a long skirt, short coat with flowered apron and headscarf, pushing a pram overflowing with holly towards the town.

Our small local Forest town Fordingbridge is a throng of activity as the festive season progresses. Outside the butcher's shop hang rows of hares, pheasants, and turkeys. Lighted Christmas trees shine above every shop and in the square people gather to sing traditional carols around a bigger lit tree. Back in the village the carol singers find their way along the dark lanes by the light of a lantern on a long pole. At one time carol singers on Christmas Eve were given a warming spiced drink. The Christmas Wassail Bowl was usually composed of strong ale, the froth of roasted apples, cloves and cinnamon, and a grate of nutmeg, ginger, and brown sugar.

Through the open doorway of the village church comes the sound of more carols sung this time to the accompaniment of the local silver band. Approaching the Church, our pathway is gilded by the glowing colours of the stained glass window.

Inside, a huge Christmas tree stands shining with coloured lights and cascades of gold and silver tinsel. Every seat is filled, and after the service coffee and sandwiches are served in the adjacent hall where everyone can meet and discuss the coming festive season.

On Christmas Eve the kitchen is a very busy place. Although the cake and puddings have been made for weeks there are still the mince-pies to make, the chestnut stuffing to mix, vegetables to prepare, the trifle to make, and the cake to decorate.

CHRISTMAS CAKE

Ten ounces of plain flour, pinch of salt, one level teaspoonful of mixed spice, half a level teaspoonful of grated nutmeg, four ounces of glace cherries, twelve ounces of seedless raisins, twelve ounces of sultanas, eight ounces of currants, eight ounces of butter, eight ounces of soft brown sugar, four eggs, two tablespoonfuls of sherry, two ounces of whole almonds, one ounce of crystallized ginger, one heaped teaspoonful of grated lemon rind, two ounces of mixed peel, chopped.

Grease a round eight inch deep cake tin. Line with two layers of greased greaseproof paper. Tie a double band of brown paper round the outside of the tin.

Pre-heat oven to 350°F and reduce to 300°F after fifteen minutes.

Sift flour, salt, spice, and nutmeg into a bowl. Wash and dry the cherries. Chop fairly finely. Clean the raisins, sultanas, and currants by putting them in a sieve with a little extra flour. Rub well until all the flour falls through the sieve, discard flour. Cream butter and brown sugar in a bowl until smooth and fluffy. Beat eggs together in a basin. Gradually beat eggs into the creamed mixture. Stir in the sherry. Put almonds into a small pan of water and bring to the boil. Drain and skin. Cut the nuts finely. Chop the ginger. Stir together ginger, almonds, cleaned fruit, cherries, lemon rind and peel. Stir fruit and nuts mixture into the sifted flour, and gradually fold into creamed mixture.

Put into prepared tin, smooth the top and make a well in centre. Cook on lower shelf of the oven for four hours. When cake is quite cold, and it should be left to cool for twelve hours, wrap in a clean cloth, then in greaseproof paper, until ready to ice.

It was once the custom in the old farmhouses to serve a dish called Frumenty for breakfast at Christmas-time.

FRUMENTY

One dish of crushed whole wheat, sugar, spice, and raisins and skimmed new milk, simmered in a jar in the oven, or at the back of the stove overnight, it can be eaten hot or cold.

On the farmsteads it is possible a fat capon was served for Christmas dinner, and most likely in some more remote cottages a joint of venison would grace the table at the Festive season.

After a traditional Christmas lunch in the middle of the day only a light tea was wanted. This was usually eaten around the open fire, and was probably just a sweet.

CHRISTMAS FIRESIDE WASSAIL BOWL
(A delicious sweet)

Half a pound of macaroons, six penny sponge cakes (trifle sponges), one ounce of powdered sugar, raisin wine, two ounces of raisins, and two pints of custard.

Crumble the macaroons and sponge cakes into a large glass dish, mix with the sugar and raisins, and saturate them thoroughly with the wine. Prepare the custard and pour over the whole of the above, stirring gently to mix perfectly. After it is cold, garnish the surface with blanched sweet almonds and glace cherries, and serve from the dish.

On Boxing Morning the New Forest pony races are held. The start is kept secret until just before-hand, only the finish is known. This is to ensure that no one can ride the course in advance. Ponies and riders gallop across the Forest and come in covered with mud but enjoying every minute of it. Watching these races can be a very chilly occupation for the spectator; we traditionally take a flask of ginger wine to keep out the cold.

OLD RECIPE FOR GINGER WINE

For the wine, use *three pounds of sugar, one lemon, three ounces of root ginger well bruised, and half a pound of stoned raisins, to the gallon of water. A quarter of a pint of brandy* may be added when the wine is finished.

Boil all the ingredients together for one hour, skimming carefully. When the liquor is quite clear, strain it into a jar or tub, and when it is cool add *a tablespoonful of dry yeast.* Stir this mixture everyday for a fortnight while adding *another half pound of raisins.* At the end of that time, strain the wine into a cask, add the brandy bottle and cork down when all hissing has ceased. It will be ready in a few weeks, but will improve if kept.

FOLLOWING a morning of standing around a good sharp walk may be needed in the afternoon to stimulate the circulation! I recall one Boxing Day walk with my husband after a heavy fall of snow. We walked across the Forest to a small wooded enclosure where we knew there was a badger sett. We found distinctive badger prints in the snow around the holes where they had come out the previous night to forage. The light was fading as we turned for home and in the holly trees silhouetted against the cold sky were redwings and fieldfare feeding on the berries.

We reached our cottage at dusk, the air chill with frost, but through the window we could see the cheering sight of the lighted Christmas tree and a blazing log fire. Inside my mother had tea ready, hot mince-pies, and a bowl of trifle in the centre of the table.

MINCEMEAT

One pound of cooking apples, one pound of currants, one pound of sultanas, one pound of raisins, one pound of chopped or shredded suet, one pound of soft brown sugar, quarter of a pound of minced candied peel, four ounces of finely minced blanched almonds, quarter of a level teaspoonful of mixed spice, half a level teaspoonful of grated nutmeg, half a lemon, one large wineglass full of brandy.

Wash and dry the fruit, cut the raisins into quarters, roughly chop the sultanas, and leave the currants whole. Peel, core, and chop the apples. Mix all the ingredients together with the brandy and the strained juice and grated rind of the half lemon. Put into a large wide mouthed jar, put a piece of greaseproof paper, cut to fit over the mincemeat and dipped in brandy, over the top. Seal the jar with two or three thicknesses of greaseproof paper and store the jar in a very cool, dry place.

MINCE PIES

Butter some tin pattypans well, and line them evenly with *fine puff paste rolled thin; fill them with mincemeat,* moisten the edges of the covers, which should be nearly quarter of an inch thick, close the pies carefully, trim off the superfluous paste, make a small aperture in the centre of the crust with the point of a knife, sugar the pies or not, at pleasure, and bake them half an hour in a well-heated but not too hot oven: lay a paper over them when they are partially done, should they appear likely to take too much colour.

TRIFLE

Line the bottom of a glass trifle dish with *sponge cakes stuck with blanched almonds; moisten with sweet wine, or with sherry and sugar.* Over these lay *a dozen ratafias.* Between these put *thin slices of citron and orange peel,* and put over these pieces of *apricot and raspberry jam with currant jelly.* Pour over *a few spoonfuls of the liquor.* The next layer should consist of *tartlet cream** about an inch thick, over which grate *some nutmeg and sprinkle a little powdered cinnamon* together with *a small quantity of lemon-peel , and some powdered loaf sugar.* Lastly top *with whipped cream* as much as the dish will contain. To decorate strew various coloured comfits over the cream.

*The tartlet cream may be made as follows:- Mix together *half a pint of cream* and *the same quantity of milk;* put into it *a piece of fresh lemon-peel or Seville orange peel and a little cinnamon, and sweeten with loaf sugar.* Let these ingredients boil for about ten minutes. Have ready prepared in another pan *the yolks of six eggs* well beaten *with a heaped teaspoonful of fine flour;* to these gradually strain ingredients, and then whisk together over a gentle fire (burner) that they may acquire the proper consistency without curdling.

It was once the custom to celebrate the "Feast Of The Stars" by holding a "Twelfth Night" party. A special cake was baked for the occasion very rich and spicy. It was iced with a blue coloured icing to represent the sky and decorated with silver stars and twelve candles.

TWELFTH NIGHT CAKE

Eight ounces of flour, four eggs, eight ounces of sugar, eight ounces of butter, one level dessertspoon of mixed spice, six ounces of currants, eight ounces of sultanas, two ounces of candied peel , two ounces of glace cherries, and a little milk to mix.

Grease a cake-tin and line with paper. Prepare the dry ingredients. Cream the butter and sugar together, beat in each egg separately, stir in the sieved flour and spice, fruit, etc., alternately with the milk, adding a little of each at a time.

Blend all the ingredients together, put into a prepared tin, and bake in a moderate oven of about 350°F for two hours. When cold, ice with pale blue icing and decorate as suggested.

HERE are three recipes from the old farmhouses which are difficult for the modern cook, but which I must add to this book for their historic value.

The old farmhouses usually had open fireplaces with wide chimneys up which the sides of bacon and hams were hung to be cured by the smoke of Forest turf or gorse wood. Most of the peasants possessed the common right of turbary which enabled them to gather fuel from the Forest in the form of peat turf and gorse wood. This fuel they burnt in their big open fire-places; or in the case of the smaller cottages in their peat stoves.

One old inn in the New Forest still has its pig-sties outside with several pigs, and inside an open fireplace with hams smoking up the chimney.

TO CURE AND SMOKE BACON

Rub the pieces of pig to be cured with rough salt, and lay in a trough for two days, then rinse well. Then rub with a mixture of salt, saltpetre and brown sugar. Turn the pieces every two days. After fourteen days take the flitches out of the pickle.

Wash the flitches in lukewarm water, then rub over with peasemeal in which a little salt has been mixed. Hang the bacon up the chimney to be smoked, burning for that purpose gorse wood.

OUR milk comes from the farm in the village, and until recently was delivered by the farmer who was in his eightieth year but always immaculate with his polished boots and gaiters.

We can see the cows as we go through the village, a handsome herd of Guernseys and Jerseys. Sometimes when the yield is low or a cow is about to calf we have to wait for our milk until second milking. When it arrives it is topped with a thick rich cream which can be taken off and used over fruit or in coffee.

The rich milk given by a cow after calving is called 'beestings'. At one time it was sought after for making a type of cheese-cake. To-day with milk being collected by tanker and taken away to be pasteurized few people would have heard of 'beestings'. Recently having discovered the old recipe for beestings cake I mentioned it to the farmer's wife, and the next morning I found a bottle of 'beestings' from a newly calved cow on my doorstep.

BEESTINGS CAKE

To a pint of beestings add a little sugar, the juice of a lemon, and put in a warm place until curdled. Mix a few currants with the curd. Line a deep baking tin with a good pastry and pour the curd into it, and bake. A little nutmeg can be grated on the top.

The last is for Miss Muffet's delight — Curds and Whey. You could try this if you are able to find some unpasteurised milk. can be bought in most pharmacies.

CURDS AND WHEY

Soak a small piece of rennet in half a teacupful of warm water, and let it remain in it for an hour or two; then pour into a quart of warm new milk a dessertspoonful of the rennet liquor, and keep it in a warm place until the whey appears separated from the curd, and looks clear. The smaller the proportion of rennet used, the more soft and delicate will be the curd.

INDEX OF RECIPES